NES
Middle Grades
Mathematics
Practice Questions

TEST PREPARATION

Dear Future Exam Success Story:

First of all, **THANK YOU** for purchasing Mometrix study materials!

Second, congratulations! You are one of the few determined test-takers who are committed to doing whatever it takes to excel on your exam. **You have come to the right place.** We developed these practice tests with one goal in mind: to deliver you the best possible approximation of the questions you will see on test day.

Standardized testing is one of the biggest obstacles on your road to success, which only increases the importance of doing well in the high-pressure, high-stakes environment of test day. Your results on this test could have a significant impact on your future, and these practice tests will give you the repetitions you need to build your familiarity and confidence with the test content and format to help you achieve your full potential on test day.

Your success is our success

We would love to hear from you! If you would like to share the story of your exam success or if you have any questions or comments in regard to our products, please contact us at **800-673-8175** or **support@mometrix.com**.

Thanks again for your business and we wish you continued success!

Sincerely,
The Mometrix Test Preparation Team

TABLE OF CONTENTS

Practice Test #1

Number Sense and Operations

1. Which of the following is closed under the operation of subtraction?

    a. whole numbers
    b. integers
    c. counting numbers
    d. natural numbers

2. Which of the following accurately describes the set of natural numbers?

    a. the set of integers
    b. the set of counting numbers, plus zero
    c. the set of numbers that may be written as the ratio of $\frac{a}{b}$, where $b \neq 0$
    d. the set of whole numbers minus zero

3. Which of the following illustrates the additive inverse property?

    a. The sum of a and 0 is a.
    b. The sum of a and $-a$ is 0.
    c. The sum of a and a is $2a$.
    d. The sum of a and any variable x is $a + x$.

4. Which of the following is an irrational number?

    a. $3.\overline{13}$
    b. $\sqrt{25}$
    c. $\frac{\pi}{2}$
    d. $\frac{37}{5}$

5. $x|y$ if

    a. $x = y \div 3$
    b. $y = x + 3$
    c. $x = y \times 3$
    d. $y = x - 3$

6. Which of the following correctly compares the sets of rational numbers and integers?

    a. The sets of rational numbers and integers are equal.
    b. The sets of rational numbers and integers are disjoint.
    c. The set of integers is a subset of the set of rational numbers.
    d. The set of rational numbers is a subset of the set of integers.

7. Which of the following statements is true?

    a. A number is divisible by 3 if the sum of the digits is divisible by 3.
    b. A number is divisible by 4 if the last digit is divisible by 2.
    c. A number is divisible by 7 if the sum of the digits is divisible by 7.
    d. A number is divisible by 6 if the sum of the last two digits is divisible by 6.

8. Which of the following correctly represents the expanded form of 0.593?

a. $5 \times \frac{1}{10^0} + 9 \times \frac{1}{10^1} + 3 \times \frac{1}{10^2}$

b. $5 \times \frac{1}{10^2} + 9 \times \frac{1}{10^3} + 3 \times \frac{1}{10^4}$

c. $5 \times \frac{1}{10^3} + 9 \times \frac{1}{10^2} + 3 \times \frac{1}{10^1}$

d. $5 \times \frac{1}{10^1} + 9 \times \frac{1}{10^2} + 3 \times \frac{1}{10^3}$

9. Quentin sets aside 10% of his monthly salary to save for a car. If his monthly salary is $2,450, how much will he set aside each month?

a. $2.45
b. $24.50
c. $245
d. $2,450

10. Nikki buys a used book that is marked down 35% from the new price. She pays 8.25% sales tax and her total cost is $9.14. What was the original price of the book?

a. $11.99
b. $12.49
c. $12.99
d. $13.49

11. Quinn deposits $250 from each quarterly paycheck into a savings account. How much is in the account after 5 years?

a. $4,800
b. $5,000
c. $5,200
d. $5,400

12. Jeni buys a phone charger for $28. If it had been marked down 30%, what was the original cost?

a. $30
b. $32
c. $35
d. $40

13. Which of the following equations may be used to convert $0.\overline{7}$ to a fraction?

a. $9x = 7.\overline{7} - 0.\overline{7}$
b. $99x = 7.\overline{7} - 0.\overline{7}$
c. $9x = 77.\overline{7} - 7.\overline{7}$
d. $90x = 7.\overline{7} - 0.\overline{7}$

14. In the base-7 number system, what is the sum of 254 and 1252?

a. 1406
b. 1506
c. 1536
d. 1596

15. Ben's current monthly rent is $750. He is moving to another apartment complex, where the monthly rent will be $900. What is the percent increase in his monthly rent amount?

   a. 15%
   b. 17.5%
   c. 19.25%
   d. 20%

16. The table below shows the amount that Kelli spent on gas in the last six months.

Month	Gas expense
January	$78.85
February	$69.49
March	$97.48
April	$82.37
May	$72.86
June	$77.91

What percentage of the total gas costs for the six months was spent in March?

   a. 17.5%
   b. 18.1%
   c. 19.9%
   d. 20.4%

17. For any natural numbers, a, b, and c, assume $a < b$ and $a < c$. Which of the following statements is *not* necessarily true?

   a. $b < c$
   b. $a < \frac{b+c}{2}$
   c. $a < bc$
   d. $2a < bc$

18. Kevin uses the pie chart below to represent how he spends his allowance. His monthly allowance is $50.

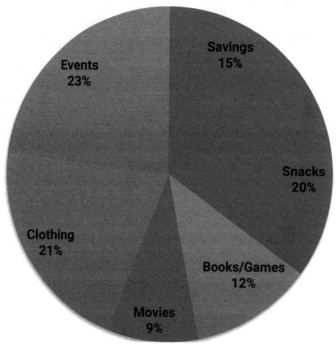

Which of the following statements is true?

    a. The amount of money he spends on snacks is more than $10.
    b. The amount of money he spends on movies, books, and games is more than $10.
    c. The amount of money he spends on savings is less than $7.
    d. The amount of money he spends on clothing and events is less than $10.

19. Olivia receives her weekly paycheck and calculates that she will spend $\frac{1}{4}$ of it on groceries. If the groceries cost $120, what is the amount of her paycheck?

    a. $360
    b. $425
    c. $480
    d. $600

20. Which of the following statements is true?

    a. The set of rational numbers is a subset of the set of natural numbers.
    b. The set of integers is a subset of the set of whole numbers.
    c. The set of natural numbers is a subset of the set of whole numbers.
    d. The set of rational numbers is a subset of the set of natural numbers.

21. Which of the following sets is *not* closed under multiplication?

    a. positive integers
    b. negative integers
    c. natural numbers
    d. whole numbers

22. Which of the following represents 88 in the base-3 system?

   a. 120
   b. 1202
   c. 10,211
   d. 10,021

23. Which expression is represented by the diagram below?

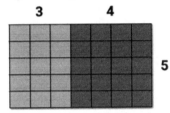

   a. $5 + (3 + 4)$
   b. $5 \times (3 \times 4)$
   c. $5 + (3 \times 4)$
   d. $5 \times (3 + 4)$

24. Meg buys a used car for $6,375. The original price had been marked down by 15%. What was the original price of the car?

   a. $7,150
   b. $7,375
   c. $7,500
   d. $7,775

25. Which of the following represents 2,417?

   a. 2.417×10^{-3}
   b. 2.417×10^{3}
   c. 24.17×10^{3}
   d. 2.417×10^{4}

Algebra and Functions

26. A car decelerates. Which of the following accurately describes the appearance of the position-time graph?

    a. It is a line with a positive slope.
    b. It is a line with a negative slope.
    c. It is a curve with an increasing slope.
    d. It is a curve with a decreasing slope.

27. Which of the following graphs does *not* represent a function?

a.
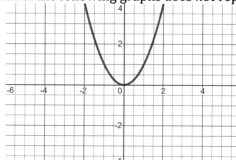

c.
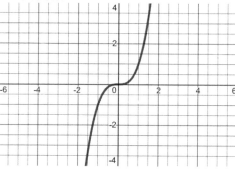

b.
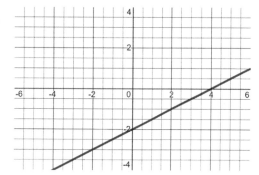

d.
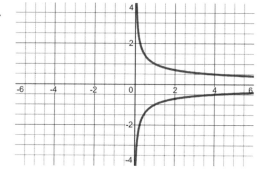

28. The variables x and y are in a linear relationship. The table below shows a few sample values. Which of the following graphs correctly represents the linear equation relating x and y?

x	y
−2	−6
−1	−4
0	−2
1	0
2	2

a.

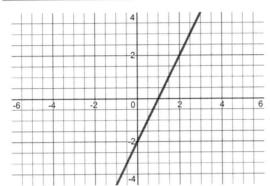

c.

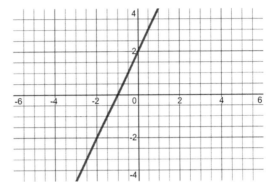

b.

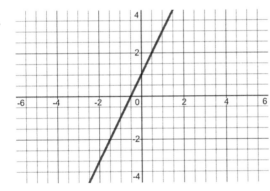

d.

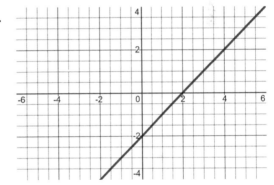

29. What is the sum of the first 35 odd, positive integers?

    a. 1,225

    b. 1,435

    c. 1,850

    d. 2,250

30. Which of the following graphs represents an inverse relationship?

a.

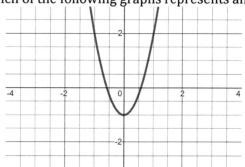

c.

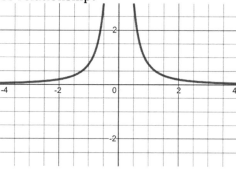

b.

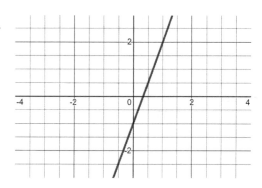

d.

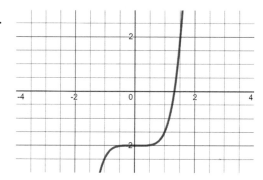

31. What is $\lim\limits_{n\to\infty}\frac{n-1}{n^2}$?

    a. 0
    b. 1
    c. 2
    d. There is no limit.

32. What linear equation includes the data in the table below?

x	y
−6	1
−2	3
4	6
8	8
10	9

    a. $y = -2x + 2$
    b. $y = -\frac{1}{2}x + 2$
    c. $y = \frac{1}{2}x + 4$
    d. $y = 2x - 2$

8

33. What is the solution to the system of linear equations graphed below?

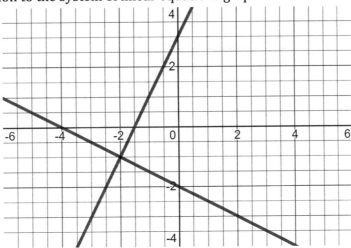

    a. $(2, -1)$
    b. $(-\frac{3}{2}, 0)$
    c. $(-2, -1)$
    d. $(-2, \frac{1}{2})$

34. What is the constant of proportionality represented by the table below?

x	y
−3	9
0	0
2	−6
7	−21
12	−36

    a. −12
    b. −9
    c. −3
    d. 3

Mometrix

35. Given the graph below, what is the average rate of change from $f(1)$ to $f(3)$?

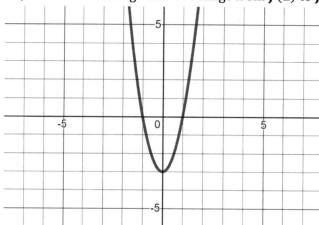

    a. 2
    b. 12
    c. 24
    d. 48

36. $g(x) = \frac{2x-3}{3-x}$. What is the equation of the horizontal asymptote?
    a. $y = -2$
    b. $y = -1$
    c. $y = \frac{2}{3}$
    d. $y = 3$

37. Which of the following graphs represents the solution to the system of inequalities below?

$$-3x + 4y \geq -4$$
$$-4x + 3y \geq -\frac{3}{2}$$

a.

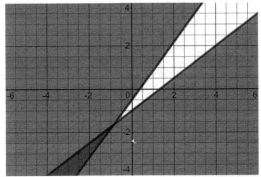

c.

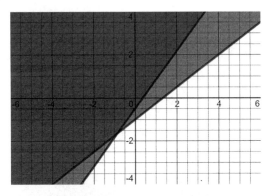

b.

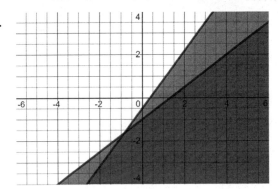

d.

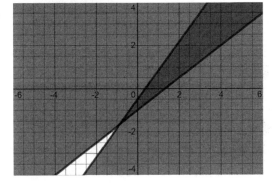

38. What is $\lim\limits_{x \to \infty} \frac{2x^3}{x^2+2}$?

  a. 0
  b. 2
  c. −2
  d. There is no limit.

39. Which of the following functions has a limit of 0?

  a. $f(x) = \frac{2x}{x^2}$
  b. $f(x) = 4x$
  c. $f(x) = \frac{x}{5}$
  d. $f(x) = \frac{3x-8}{x}$

40. Becca needs to order 8 sandwiches for her team lunch and she knows they will cost at least $40. Which of the following inequalities represents the possible costs?

  a. $40 \geq 8s$
  b. $40 < 8s$
  c. $40 > 8s$
  d. $40 \leq 8s$

11

41. Which of the following represents a proportional relationship?

a.
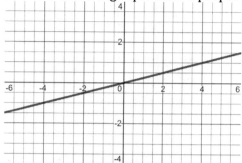

c.
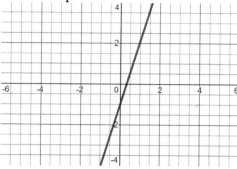

b.
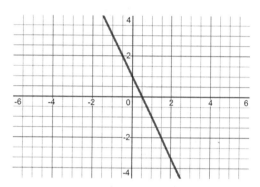

d.
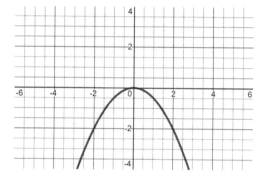

42. Which of the following graphs represents the solution to $y \leq \frac{1}{2}x - 2$?

a.
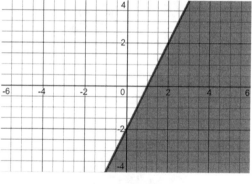

c.
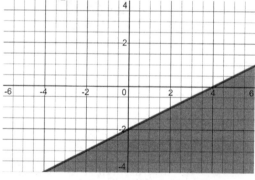

b.
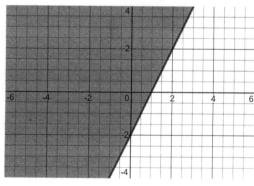

d.
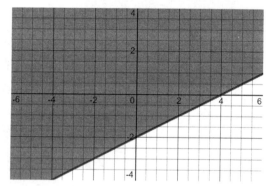

43. Lilia needs to buy envelopes and stamps. Each box of envelopes costs $2.50. Each book of stamps costs $6.00. She intends to spend no more than $30. Which of the following graphs represents the possible combinations of stamps and envelopes that she may purchase, if the y-axis represents books of stamps and the x-axis represents boxes of envelopes?

a.

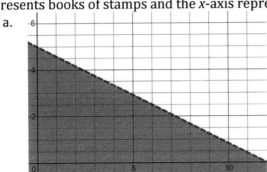

c.

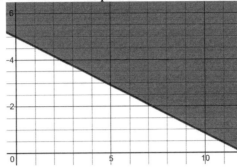

b.

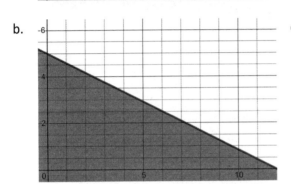

d.

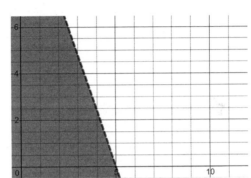

44. Which of the following represents an inverse proportional relationship?

a. $y = -7x$

b. $y = \frac{1}{7}x$

c. $y = -\frac{7}{x}$

d. $y = 7x^2$

45. Luke's monthly cell phone cost is represented by the graph shown below. The x-axis represents the number of months since purchasing the phone plan and the y-axis represents the total cost paid up to that point. Which of the following statements is correct?

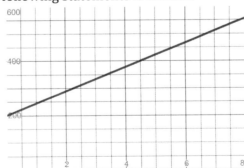

a. The cost is linear, but not proportional.

b. The cost is linear and proportional.

c. The cost is proportional, but not linear.

d. The cost represents an inverse proportional relationship.

13

Mometrix

46. Which of the following represents a function?

    a. {(2, 1), (3, –2), (6, 8), (–1, –4), (4, –1)}
    b. {(8, 5), (7, 9), (3, 1), (4, 7), (3, 6)}
    c. {(–4, 6), (2, 3), (4, –2), (3, 6), (–4, 2)}
    d. {(2, 6), (6, 1), (5, 8), (2, –1), (–3, 1)}

47. Which of the following tables contains points in an exponential function?

a.

x	y
–3	9
–1	–3
0	0
2	6
5	15

c.

x	y
–2	1/9
0	1
1	3
3	27
6	729

b.

x	y
–2	4
0	0
3	6
6	24
8	48

d.

x	y
–1	0
2	5
4	9
5	11
7	15

48. Which of the following expressions is equivalent to $-2x(x + 6)^2$?

    a. $-2x^3 + 12x^2 - 36x$
    b. $-2x^3 - 24x^2 - 72x$
    c. $-2x^2 + 36x$
    d. $-2x^3 - 12x^2 - 72x$

49. What is $\lim\limits_{n \to \infty} \frac{3-4n}{n}$?

    a. –16
    b. –4
    c. 3
    d. There is no limit.

50. What is the derivative of $f(x) = 3x^5$?

    a. $3x$
    b. $3x^4$
    c. $15x$
    d. $15x^4$

51. Which of the following functions converges?

    a. $f(x) = \frac{3x^2}{2x}$
    b. $f(x) = 12 - \frac{7x^2}{x^2}$
    c. $f(x) = 7x$
    d. $f(x) = \frac{x^2+2}{x}$

14

Copyright © Mometrix Media. You have been licensed one copy of this document for personal use only. Any other reproduction or redistribution is strictly prohibited. All rights reserved.

52. $f(x) = \frac{2-x}{4x}$. What is the equation of the horizontal asymptote?

    a. $y = -\frac{1}{4}$

    b. $y = -\frac{1}{2}$

    c. $y = -2$

    d. $y = 2$

53. Lucy has $25 and needs to buy pens, highlighters, and notebooks. Each pack of pens costs $4. Each pack of highlighters costs $5. Each notebook costs $1.50. Which of the following inequalities may be used to find the combinations of pens, highlighters, and notebooks that she may purchase?

    a. $4p + 5h + 1.5n > 25$

    b. $4p + 5h + 1.5n < 25$

    c. $4p + 5h + 1.5n \leq 25$

    d. $4p + 5h + 1.5n \geq 25$

54. Raquel pays $12 per ticket to the fair, plus an $8 parking fee. Which of the following equations represents the cost?

    a. $y = 8x + 12$

    b. $y = 20x$

    c. $y = 12x + 8$

    d. $y = 12x + 20$

55. Which of the following is the graph of the equation $y = -\frac{1}{2}x + 2$?

a.
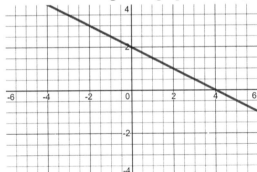

c.
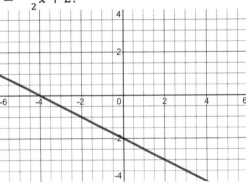

b.
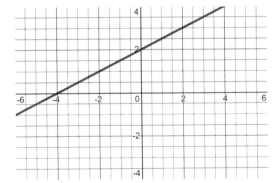

d.
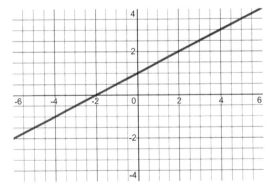

56. Which type of function is represented by the table of values below?

x	y
−2	8
−1	2
0	0
1	2
2	8

    a. linear
    b. quadratic
    c. cubic
    d. exponential

57. The expression $3x^2 + 3x - 18$ is equal to the product of $(x + 3)$ and which other factor?
    a. $(3x - 4)$
    b. $(3x - 6)$
    c. $(3x + 4)$
    d. $(3x + 6)$

58. Which of the following formulas may be used to represent the sequence $-1, 6, 13, 20, 27, ...$?
    a. $a_n = 7n - 8; n \in \mathbb{N}$
    b. $a_n = n - 7; n \in \mathbb{N}$
    c. $a_n = n - 8; n \in \mathbb{N}$
    d. $a_n = 7n - 1; n \in \mathbb{N}$

59. Which of the following formulas may be used to represent the sequence $9, 27, 81, 243, ...$?
    a. $y = 3x+6$
    b. $y = x + 9$
    c. $y = 3^{x+1}$
    d. $y = (x + 1)^3$

60. Gillian works out for 15 minutes a day for the first month. During each subsequent month, she plans to exercise an additional 5 minutes per day as the previous month. Which of the following equations represents the amount she will work out each day during the nth month?
    a. $a_n = 15n - 5$
    b. $a_n = 15n + 1$
    c. $a_n = 5n + 10$
    d. $a_n = 5n + 15$

61. Julia drops a ball from a second-story window. The height of the ball is modeled by the function $f(x) = -2.5x^2 + 2x + 9$, where $f(x)$ represents the height of the ball and x represents the number of seconds. Which of the following best represents the number of seconds that will pass before the ball reaches the ground?
    a. 2.1
    b. 2.3
    c. 2.5
    d. 2.8

62. Which of the following represents the graph of $y = (x + 2)^2 - 3$?

a.
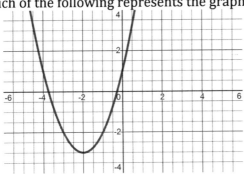

c.
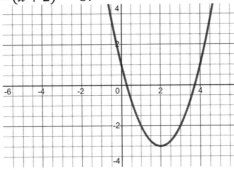

b.
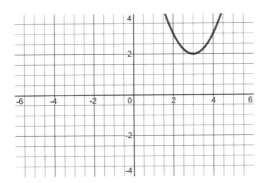

d.
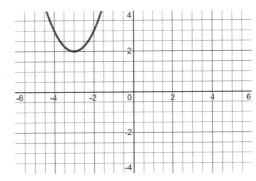

63. The graph of the parent function $y = x^2$ is shifted 4 units to the right and 6 units down. Which of the following equations represents the transformed function?

    a. $y = (x - 4)^2 - 6$
    b. $y = (x + 4)^2 - 6$
    c. $y = (x - 4)^2 + 6$
    d. $y = (x + 4)^2 + 6$

64. What is the derivative of $g(x) = x^{2yz}$?

    a. $2yz \times x^{yz}$
    b. $yz \times x^{2yz-1}$
    c. $2yz \times x^{2yz-1}$
    d. $yz \times x^{yz}$

17

65. Which of the following equations represents a line parallel to the one graphed below and passing through the point (−2, 1)?

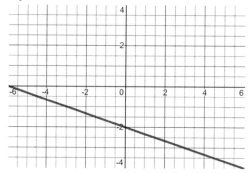

a. $y = -\frac{1}{3}x - 2$

b. $y = -\frac{1}{3}x + \frac{1}{3}$

c. $y = 3x + 7$

d. $y = 3x - 2$

66. Which of the following equations represents a line perpendicular to the one graphed below and passing through the point (1, −2)?

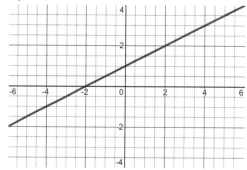

a. $y = \frac{1}{2}x + 1$

b. $y = \frac{1}{2}x - 1$

c. $y = -2x + \frac{1}{2}$

d. $y = -2x$

67. Sheila eats $\frac{1}{3}$ of a chocolate bar. Then, she eats an additional area $\frac{1}{3}$ the size of what she just ate. Next, she eats another area $\frac{1}{3}$ as large as the previous one. As she continues the process to infinity, what is the limit of the amount of the chocolate bar she eats?

a. $\frac{1}{3}$

b. $\frac{2}{3}$

c. $\frac{3}{4}$

d. $\frac{1}{2}$

68. Matt can finish the dishes in 15 minutes. Quinn can finish them in 20 minutes. If they work together, approximately how long will it take them to finish the dishes?

    a. 5.8 minutes
    b. 6.4 minutes
    c. 7.3 minutes
    d. 8.6 minutes

69. Laura buys 6 pens and 2 notebooks for $7.20. Julio buys 15 pens and 1 notebook for $12.60. How much does one notebook cost?

    a. $0.50
    b. $0.75
    c. $1.35
    d. $1.50

70. What is $\lim\limits_{x \to \frac{1}{2}}(8x^2 - 6x + 3)$?

    a. $-\dfrac{1}{2}$
    b. 0
    c. 2
    d. 4

71. Myles has a $60 budget to purchase a team lunch. He plans to buy sandwiches and salads. He needs to purchase a minimum of 15 items to make sure everyone has food. Each sandwich costs $3 and each salad costs $5. Which of the following graphs correctly shows the possible combinations of sandwiches and salads that he may buy, assuming that the x-axis represents sandwiches and the y-axis represents salads?

a.
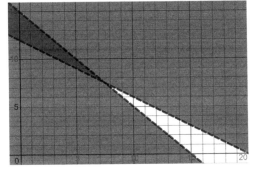

c.
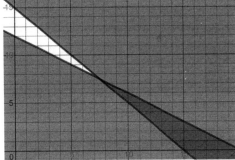

b.
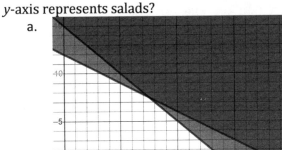

d.
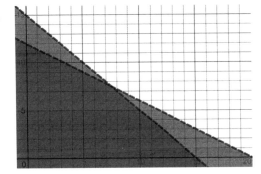

72. If $f(x) = \frac{x^3+3x+2}{2x}$, what is $f(-1)$?

    a. -2

    b. $\frac{1}{2}$

    c. 1

    d. -1

73. The initial term of a sequence is 5. Each term in the sequence is $\frac{3}{5}$ the amount of the previous term. What is the sum of the terms, as n approaches infinity?

    a. 5

    b. 8

    c. 12.5

    d. 15.75

74. Lynn picked two tomatoes out of her garden the first week they began producing. For each subsequent week, she picked three times as many as the week before, while the plants were in season. Which of the following equations represents the amount she saved during the nth week?

    a. $a_n = 2 + 3^n$

    b. $a_n = 2 \times 3^{n-1}$

    c. $a_n = 2 \times 3^n$

    d. $a_n = 3n - 2$

75. What is the solution to the system of linear equations below?

$$2x - 3y = 24$$
$$5x + 6y = -21$$

    a. $(-6, 3)$

    b. $(-3, -10)$

    c. $(3, -6)$

    d. $(6, -4)$

Measurement and Geometry

76. How many square inches of paper would it take to wrap a ball with a radius of 0.8 feet?

    a. 8.04

    b. 59.72

    c. 437.96

    d. 1,157.76

77. Which of the following represents the net of a square pyramid?

a.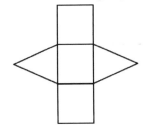

c.

b.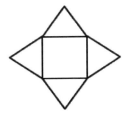

d.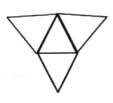

78. What is the slope of the hypotenuse in the triangle graphed below?

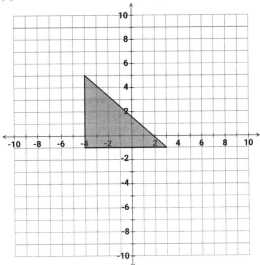

a. $-\dfrac{6}{7}$

b. $-\dfrac{7}{6}$

c. $\dfrac{6}{7}$

d. $\dfrac{7}{6}$

21

79. Which of the following steps were applied to the quadrangle in Quadrant I?

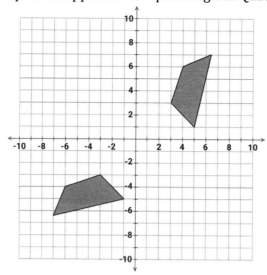

    a. reflection across the y-axis and rotation of 90 degrees
    b. reflection across the x-axis and rotation of 180 degrees
    c. reflection across the x-axis and rotation of 270 degrees
    d. reflection across the y-axis and rotation of 180 degrees

80. A room has a length of 12 feet, a height of 9 feet, and a width of 10 feet. How many square feet are there to paint, including walls, floor, and ceiling?
    a. 425
    b. 636
    c. 898
    d. 1,080

81. What is the value of x, shown in the diagram below?

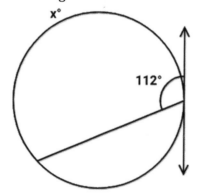

    a. 56
    b. 112
    c. 224
    d. 318

82. Which of the following shapes is *not* a possible cross-section of a triangular prism?

 a. circle
 b. rectangle
 c. trapezoid
 d. triangle

83. What is the area of the figure graphed below?

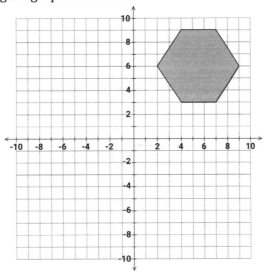

 a. 15 units^2
 b. 25 units^2
 c. 27.5 units^2
 d. 30 units^2

84. Each base of a triangular prism has a base length of 7.5 cm and a height of 10 cm. The height of the prism is 12 cm. What is the volume of the prism?

 a. 375 cm^3
 b. 450 cm^3
 c. 525 cm^3
 d. 600 cm^3

85. A lotion pump is in the shape of a square pyramid. If the base has a side length of 3.5 inches and the height of the container is 6 inches, how many cubic inches of lotion can the container hold?

 a. 18.6
 b. 24.5
 c. 28.9
 d. 32.5

86. What is the distance on a coordinate plane from (−4, 8) to (8, −3)?

 a. $\sqrt{41}$
 b. $\sqrt{137}$
 c. $\sqrt{265}$
 d. $\sqrt{329}$

87. A 12-foot-tall tree casts a shadow that is 9.8 ft in length. Which of the following best represents the distance from the top of the tree to the end of the shadow?

    a. 6.9 ft
    b. 12.8 ft
    c. 15.5 ft
    d. 18.5 ft

88. Which of the following measurements is the best approximation of 17.85 square feet?

    a. 2,385 in^2
    b. 2,425 in^2
    c. 2,570 in^2
    d. 2,690 in^2

89. Given the diagram below, which of the following theorems may be used to verify that lines a and b are parallel?

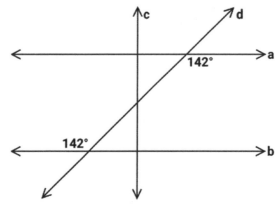

    a. Alternate Interior Angles Converse Theorem
    b. Alternate Exterior Angles Converse Theorem
    c. Consecutive Interior Angles Converse Theorem
    d. Corresponding Angles Converse Theorem

90. Zel drinks $\frac{1}{8}$ of a glass of juice. If the glass contains $6\frac{2}{3}$ fluid ounces of juice, how much does she drink?

    a. $\frac{7}{24}$ fluid ounces
    b. $\frac{5}{6}$ fluid ounces
    c. $\frac{1}{3}$ fluid ounces
    d. $\frac{3}{4}$ fluid ounces

91. The figure on the graph below represents a triangular path, beginning and ending at point *x*. If each unit represents 3.5 miles, which of the following best represents the total distance of the path?

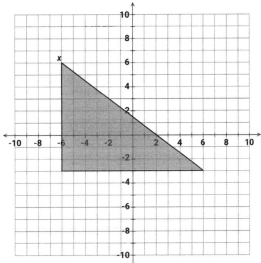

    a. 36 miles
    b. 57.5 miles
    c. 108 miles
    d. 126 miles

92. A can has a diameter of 4 inches and a height of 4.5 inches. Which of the following best represents the volume of the can?
    a. 56.5 in^3
    b. 72.8 in^3
    c. 135.6 in^3
    d. 226.1 in^3

93. What is the length of the hypotenuse in the right triangle shown below?

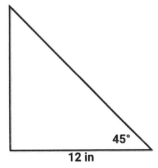

    a. 15 in
    b. 12$\sqrt{3}$ in
    c. 18 in
    d. 12$\sqrt{2}$ in

94. Given the diagram below, what is the measure of $\overset{\frown}{AC}$?

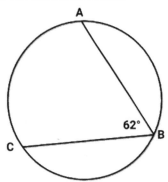

a. 31°
b. 62°
c. 124°
d. 208°

95. A convex three-dimensional figure has 12 edges and 8 vertices. How many faces does it have?

a. 4
b. 5
c. 6
d. 8

96. What is the approximate area of the shaded region in the figure shown below?

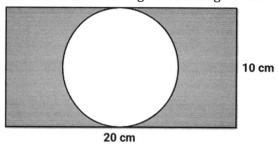

10 cm

20 cm

a. 122 cm²
b. 144 cm²
c. 176 cm²
d. 193 cm²

97. Which of the following transformations has been applied to the shaded triangle?

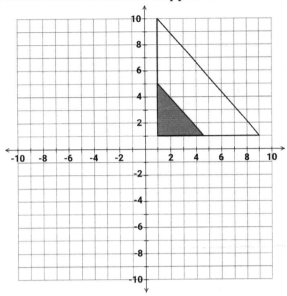

    a. translation
    b. rotation of 90 degrees
    c. reflection
    d. dilation

98. Which of the following best represents the measurement of x, shown in the right triangle below?

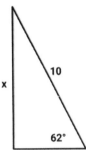

    a. 5.6
    b. 6.4
    c. 7.9
    d. 8.8

99. A city is at an elevation of 4,900 feet. Which of the following best represents the elevation in miles?

    a. 0.93 miles
    b. 0.98 miles
    c. 1.08 miles
    d. 1.21 miles

100. A ball has a radius of 2.75 inches. Which of the following best represents the volume?

    a. 79.9 in^3
    b. 87.1 in^3
    c. 96.5 in^3
    d. 104.3 in^3

101. A 20-foot flagpole casts a shadow that is 15 feet in length. How long is the shadow cast by a 5-foot person standing next to the flagpole?

    a. 1.75 feet
    b. 2.5 feet
    c. 3.25 feet
    d. 3.75 feet

102. What is the perimeter of the trapezoid graphed below?

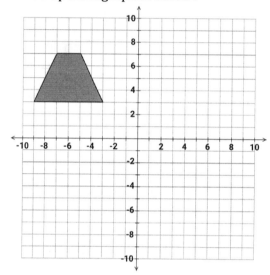

    a. $6 + \sqrt{10}$
    b. $8 + 4\sqrt{5}$
    c. $8 + 2\sqrt{5}$
    d. $7 + 2\sqrt{10}$

103. Which of the following pairs of shapes may tessellate a plane?

    a. equilateral triangles and squares
    b. regular pentagons and equilateral triangles
    c. regular pentagons and squares
    d. regular octagons and equilateral triangles

104. What is the value of **x**, shown in the diagram below?

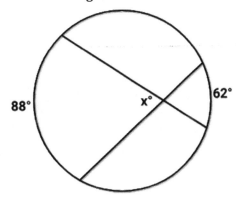

88°   x°   62°

    a. 13
    b. 58
    c. 75
    d. 150

105. Given that the two horizontal lines in the diagram below are parallel, which pair of angles is congruent?

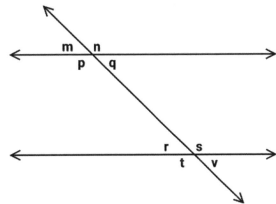

m n
p q

r s
t v

    a. ∠n and ∠s
    b. ∠m and ∠p
    c. ∠q and ∠s
    d. ∠s and ∠v

106. What scale factor was applied to the larger triangle to obtain the smaller triangle below?

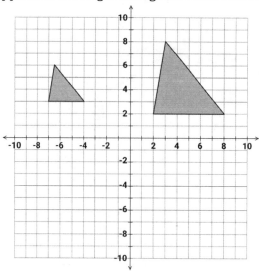

a. $\frac{1}{4}$
b. $\frac{1}{3}$
c. $\frac{1}{2}$
d. $\frac{2}{3}$

107. What is the midpoint of the line segment below?

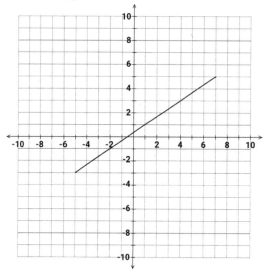

a. (−0.5, 2)
b. (1, 1)
c. (1.5, 3)
d. (2, 1.5)

30

108. The two triangles shown below are similar (units are inches). What is the measurement of x?

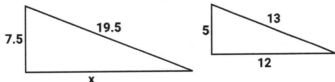

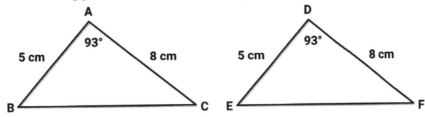

a. 12.5 in
b. 18 in
c. 21.25 in
d. 24 in

109. Which of the following postulates proves the congruence of the triangles below?

a. ASA
b. AAS
c. SAS
d. SSS

110. Which of the following pairs of equations represents the lines of symmetry in the figure below?

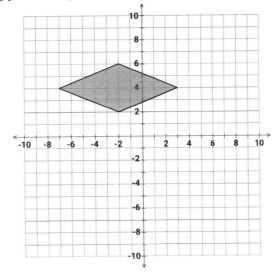

a. $x = -2, y = 4$
b. $x = 2, y = 4$
c. $y = -2, x = 4$
d. $y = 2, x = 4$

111. Which of the following postulates may be used to prove the similarity of ΔMNP and ΔQNR?

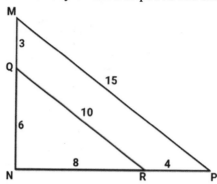

    a. ASA
    b. AA
    c. AAS
    d. SSS

112. Given that the two horizontal lines in the diagram below are parallel, which of the following statements is correct?

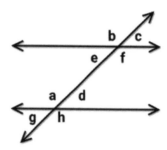

    a. ∠b and ∠f are complementary.
    b. ∠e and ∠c are supplementary.
    c. ∠a and ∠b are supplementary.
    d. ∠c and ∠d are congruent.

Statistics, Probability, and Discrete Mathematics

113. Using logic, when is $p \wedge q$ false?

    I. When both p and q are true.
    II. When p is true but q is false.
    III. When q is true but p is false.

  a. I only
  b. II and III only
  c. III only
  d. I, II, and III

114. Will tosses a coin 250 times. How many times can he expect to get tails?

  a. 75
  b. 100
  c. 125
  d. 150

115. Which of the following represents a tautology?

  a. $(p \wedge q) \rightarrow p$
  b. $(q \wedge p) \rightarrow p$
  c. $(p \vee q) \rightarrow p$
  d. $(q \vee p) \rightarrow p$

116. $A = \{3, -2, 7\}$ and $B = \{-3, 5, 6, 2\}$. What is $A \cap B$?

  a. $\{-3, -2, 2, 3, 5, 6, 7\}$
  b. $\{2, 3\}$
  c. $\{-3, -2, 2, 3\}$
  d. $\emptyset$

117. How many ways can you arrange the letters below, if order does not matter?

    PIZZA

  a. 30
  b. 60
  c. 90
  d. 120

118. For which of the following data sets would the mean be an appropriate measure of center to use?

  a. 7, 7, 9, 10, 10, 11, 13, 14, 46, 50
  b. 6, 8, 11, 15, 17, 17, 21, 22, 25, 25
  c. 4, 9, 36, 41, 43, 44, 48, 48, 49, 50
  d. 2, 91, 92, 96, 96, 98, 100, 102, 104, 105

119. Alicia rolls a standard six-sided die. What is the probability she rolls a number greater than or equal to 3?

   a. $\frac{5}{6}$

   b. $\frac{3}{5}$

   c. $\frac{3}{4}$

   d. $\frac{2}{3}$

120. A student scores 92 on a final exam. The class average is 86, with a standard deviation of 2.5 points. How many standard deviations above the class average is the student's score?

   a. 1.6
   b. 2
   c. 2.4
   d. 2.8

121. What is the interquartile range of the data below?

      4, 7, 7, 9, 11, 14, 17, 18, 18, 23

   a. 10
   b. 11
   c. 12
   d. 13

122. Which of the following describes a sampling technique that will likely increase the sampling error?

   a. alphabetizing names on a list and choosing every other name
   b. using a larger sample size
   c. replicating the study with new groups
   d. grouping a sample according to age and choosing the first 50 people

123. A student scores 70 on a test. The class average is 85, with a standard deviation of 5 points. What percentage of the class scored below this student?

   a. 0.13%
   b. 0.85%
   c. 1.42%
   d. 2.28%

124. A student scores 71 on a final exam. Another student scores 86 on the exam. The class average is 81, with a standard deviation of 10 points. What percentage of the class scored within the range of these two students' scores?

   a. 53.28%
   b. 58.94%
   c. 64.11%
   d. 71.28%

125. What is the area under the normal curve between ±2.5 standard deviations?

    a. approximately 68%
    b. approximately 90%
    c. approximately 95%
    d. approximately 99%

126. If the *x*-axis in the scatter plot below represents the number of items sold and the *y*-axis represents the total profit in dollars, which of the following is the *best* estimate for the profit received for selling 15 items?

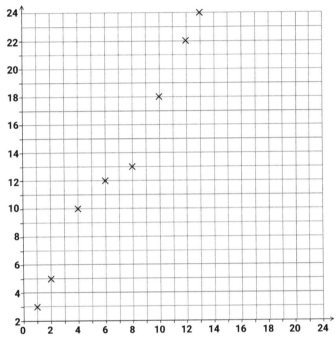

    a. $24
    b. $27
    c. $30
    d. $33

127. How many ways can the numerals 1–8 be arranged?

    a. 5,040
    b. 40,320
    c. 362,880
    d. 3,628,800

128. What is the limit of the series below?

$$1 + \frac{1}{3} + \frac{1}{9} + \frac{1}{27} + \frac{1}{81} + \cdots$$

    a. 2
    b. $1\frac{3}{4}$
    c. $1\frac{1}{2}$
    d. $1\frac{5}{6}$

129. Using logic, when is $p \vee q$ true?

    I. When both p and q are true.
    II. When either p or q is true, but not both.
    III. When both p and q are false.

  a. I only
  b. III only
  c. I and II only
  d. I, II, and III

130. Eliza rolls a die. What is the probability she gets a 6 or an even number?

  a. $\frac{1}{4}$
  b. $\frac{1}{2}$
  c. $\frac{2}{3}$
  d. $\frac{3}{4}$

131. Erika must choose her outfit from 4 pairs of jeans, 6 tops, and 5 pairs of shoes. How many possible outfits may she create with one item from each category?

  a. 12
  b. 24
  c. 60
  d. 120

132. A company claims that the average hourly wage of its employees is $27. A random sample of 25 employees shows a wage mean of $26.50 and a standard deviation of $1.50. Which of the following statements is true?

  a. The company's claim is likely true, as evidenced by a p-value less than 0.05.
  b. The company's claim is likely false, as evidenced by a p-value less than 0.05.
  c. The company's claim is likely true, as evidenced by a p-value greater than 0.05.
  d. The company's claim is likely false, as evidenced by a p-value greater than 0.05.

133. $A = \{6, 4, -3, 1, 6, 0\}$ and $B = \{-1, 2, 3, 9, 0\}$. What is $A \cup B$?

  a. $\{0\}$
  b. $\{-3, -1, 0, 1, 2, 3, 4, 6, 9\}$
  c. $\emptyset$
  d. $\{1, 3, 4, 6, 9\}$

134. A student scores 72 on a test. The class average is 84, with a standard deviation of 8 points. What percentage of the class scored above this student?

  a. 77.59%
  b. 82.56%
  c. 89.78%
  d. 93.32%

135. What is the size of the sample space for tossing five coins?

    a. 8
    b. 16
    c. 32
    d. 64

136. A box of crackers states that there are approximately 150 crackers in the box. A random sample of 25 boxes shows a mean of 146 crackers, with a standard deviation of 3 crackers. Which of the following statements is correct?

    a. The manufacturer's claim is likely true, as evidenced by a p-value less than 0.01.
    b. The manufacturer's claim is likely true, as evidenced by a p-value greater than 0.01.
    c. The manufacturer's claim is likely false, as evidenced by a p-value less than 0.01.
    d. The manufacturer's claim is likely false, as evidenced by a p-value greater than 0.01.

137. Which of the following best represents the standard deviation of the data below?

        8, 10, 11, 13, 13, 16, 17, 20

    a. 2.9
    b. 3.4
    c. 4.0
    d. 4.6

138. $A = \{4, 1, 7, 3, -2, 2\}$ and $B = \{2, 0, 1, 4, 6, 8\}$. What is $A \cap B$?

    a. $\{-2, 0, 1, 2, 3, 4, 6, 7, 8\}$
    b. $\{1, 2, 4\}$
    c. $\emptyset$
    d. $\{0, 2\}$

139. Which of the following statements is *not* true?

    a. In a negatively skewed distribution, the tail is on the left.
    b. In a positively skewed distribution, the median is greater than the mode.
    c. In a normal distribution, the mean is at the peak.
    d. In a positively skewed distribution, the median is closer to the third quartile than the first.

140. Lewis rolls a die and tosses a coin. What is the probability he gets a number less than 3 and heads?

    a. $\frac{1}{6}$
    b. $\frac{1}{4}$
    c. $\frac{1}{3}$
    d. 1

141. 225 students are surveyed. 95 of the students like only coffee. 30 of the students like only tea. 55 of the students like both coffee and tea. How many students like neither coffee nor tea?

    a. 25
    b. 35
    c. 45
    d. 55

142. Given the two-way frequency table below, which of the following *best* represents P(bowl or chicken soup)?

	Chicken Soup	Vegetable Soup	Total
Cup	329	248	577
Bowl	642	591	1233
Total	971	839	1810

a. 70%
b. 75%
c. 80%
d. 85%

143. A cereal manufacturer claims to include 16 ounces in each container, with a standard deviation of 0.2 ounces. A random sample of 30 containers shows a mean of 16.1 ounces. Which of the following statements is true?

a. The manufacturer's claim is likely true, as evidenced by a p-value less than 0.05.
b. The manufacturer's claim is likely true, as evidenced by a p-value greater than 0.05.
c. The manufacturer's claim is likely false, as evidenced by a p-value less than 0.05.
d. The manufacturer's claim is likely false, as evidenced by a p-value greater than 0.05.

144. What is the converse of the statement below?

If it is Saturday, Joe buys a donut.

a. If it is not Saturday, Joe does not buy a donut.
b. If it is Saturday, Joe buys a donut.
c. If Joe buys a donut, it is Saturday.
d. If Joe does not buy a donut, it is not Saturday.

145. Dan rolls a die and tosses a coin. What is the probability he gets a non-prime number or tails?

a. $\frac{1}{2}$
b. $\frac{2}{3}$
c. $\frac{3}{4}$
d. $\frac{5}{6}$

146. Which of the following is logically equivalent to $\neg q \to \neg p$?

a. $q \to p$
b. $\neg p \to \neg q$
c. $p \to q$
d. $p \land q$

147. What is the contrapositive of the statement below?

If Bryan eats peanuts, he has an allergic reaction.

a. If Bryan eats peanuts, he does not have an allergic reaction.
b. If Bryan does not have an allergic reaction, he does not eat peanuts.
c. If Bryan does not eat peanuts, he does not have an allergic reaction.
d. If Bryan does not eat peanuts, he has an allergic reaction.

148. Class A, with a total of 32 students, had a final exam average of 87 and a standard deviation of 3.5 points. Class B, with a total of 25 students, had a final exam average of 89, with a standard deviation of 2.5 points. Which of the following statements is true?

a. There is no significant difference between the classes, as evidenced by a p-value greater than 0.05.
b. There is no significant difference between the classes, as evidenced by a p-value less than 0.05.
c. There is a significant difference between the classes, as evidenced by a p-value greater than 0.05.
d. There is a significant difference between the classes, as evidenced by a p-value less than 0.05.

149. How many ways can the 1st–4th place finishers be selected from 7 competitors?

a. 120
b. 360
c. 720
d. 840

150. Given the boxplots below, which of the following statements is correct?

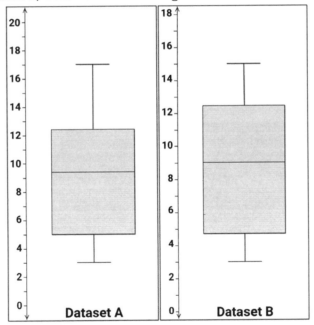

a. Dataset A has a larger range and a larger median.
b. Dataset A has a smaller range and a larger median.
c. Dataset A has a larger range and a smaller median.
d. Dataset A has a smaller range and a smaller median.

Constructed Response

1. Michael buys a new laptop for $1,850. The computer loses 10% of its value the day it is purchased and depreciates at a constant rate following that. The value of the computer as a function of time can be modeled by $y = c - 0.03cx$, where y is the value of the laptop x months after it was purchased and c is the value after the initial 10% depreciation.

    a. What is the value of the laptop 1 year after its purchase date? Show your work.

    b. On an xy-grid, graph the value, y, of the computer, as a function of x, where x represents the number of months after the purchase date, for $0 \le x \le 9$ months. Label the axes and show the scales used for the graph.

    c. Use your graph to estimate the number of months, x, after the purchase date that the value of the laptop is $1,500. Label this point on your graph and indicate the approximate coordinates of the point.

    d. Algebraically find the number of months, x, after the purchase date that the value of the laptop is exactly $1,500. Round your solution to the nearest tenth of a month. Show your work.

2. Gillian is planning a festival in her city square. The circular area below is the part of the square with available electricity and has been set aside for food vendors. There will be four square vendor spaces, each with a side of 10 feet, within the circular area (which has a diameter of 30 feet).

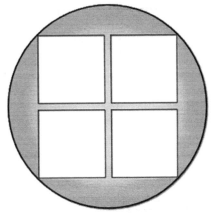

a. According to the diagram, what is the area, in square feet, that will be taken up by the vendors? Show your work.

b. According to the diagram, what percentage of the circle will be available for customers to walk among the vendors? Show your work.

c. If a random point is chosen within the circular area, what is the probability that it would fall in a vendor's booth? Show your work or explain your reasoning.

3. Below are listed the weights in pounds of the 16 students in a fourth grade class.

51, 54, 54, 56, 59, 60, 62, 63, 64, 64, 67, 69, 69, 73, 76, 83

a. For the numbers above, define and identify the median and the range.

b. Define and calculate the mean for the list of numbers above.

c. Draw a stem and leaf plot of the data using the tens digits as the stems and the units digits as the leaves.

Answer Key and Explanations

Number Sense and Operations

1. B: Subtracting an integer from another integer will always result in an integer.

2. D: The set of natural numbers is represented as $\{0, 1, 2, 3, \dots\}$, also known as counting numbers. The set of whole numbers includes all natural numbers, plus zero. Thus, the set of natural numbers contains the whole numbers minus zero.

3. B: The additive inverse property states: the sum of a number and its negative value is 0.

4. C: The decimal expansion of an irrational number does not terminate or repeat. The number π is considered irrational because it does not terminate or repeat.

5. A: $x|y$ means that y is divisible by x: that is, that y is equal to the product of x and any constant such as 3.

6. C: The set of integers is represented as $\{\dots -3, -2, -1, 0, 1, 2, 3, \dots\}$. The set of rational numbers includes all of these as well as any number that can be represented as a fraction of two integers, where the denominator is not zero. So the set of integers is a subset of the set of rational numbers.

7. A: If the digits in a number add up to a multiple of 3, it is also divisible by 3. For instance, in the number 27, $2 + 7 = 9$, which is a multiple of 3.

8. D: The 5 is in the tenths place, the 9 in the hundredths place, and the 3 in the thousandths place. Thus, 0.593 is equal to the sum of the product of 5 and $\frac{1}{10}$, the product of 9 and $\frac{1}{100}$, and the product of 3 and $\frac{1}{1000}$.

9. C: The amount he saves is equal to 0.1(2,450). Thus, he saves $245.

10. C: The original price may be modeled by the equation, $(x - 0.35x) + 0.0825(x - 0.35x) = 9.14$, which simplifies to $0.703625x = 9.14$. Dividing each side of the equation by the coefficient of x gives $x \approx 12.99$.

11. B: There are 60 months in 5 years. Since a quarter is 3 months, the following proportion may be written: $\frac{250}{3} = \frac{x}{60}$. We cross-multiply to obtain the equation $3x = 15{,}000$. Dividing both sides of the equation by 3 gives $x = 5{,}000$.

12. D: The original cost may be represented by the equation $28 = x - 0.3x$ or $28 = 0.7x$. Dividing both sides of the equation by 0.7 gives $x = 40$.

13. A: The repeating decimal may be converted to a fraction by writing:

$$10x = 7.\overline{7}$$
$$-\quad\ x = 0.\overline{7}$$

which simplifies as $10x - x = 7.\overline{7} - 0.\overline{7}$, or $9x = 7.\overline{7} - 0.\overline{7}$.

14. C: The sum is written as:

$$
\begin{array}{r}
1252 \\
+ \ 254 \\
\hline
1536
\end{array}
$$

The sum of 5 and 5 equals 10. In the base-7 number system, a number cannot contain any number larger than 6, so we rewrite it as 13 (1 seven plus 3 ones) and carry the 1 to the next column to the left. The remaining digits can all be added normally without exceeding 6.

15. D: The percent increase is represented as $\frac{900-750}{750}$, which equals 0.2 or 20%.

16. D: The total gas cost is $478.96. Thus, the ratio $\frac{97.48}{478.96}$ represents the percentage of gas cost spent in March. $\frac{97.48}{478.96} \approx 0.204$ or 20.4%.

17. A: If $a < b$ and $a < c$, it does not necessary follow that $b < c$. For example, a could equal 3, b could equal 5, and c could equal 4.

18. B: The amount he spends on movies, books, and games is equal to 0.21(50), or $10.50, which is more than $10.

19. C: Olivia's paycheck may be modeled as $\frac{1}{4}x = 120$. Multiplying both sides of the equation by 4 gives $x = 480$.

20. C: The set of natural numbers is contained within the set of whole numbers, and is hence a subset. Whole numbers include all positive integers plus zero, while natural numbers include all positive integers but not zero.

21. B: Multiplying two negative integers will result in a positive integer, which is not in the set of negative integers.

22. D: First divide 3 into 88, recording the remainder. Then divide 3 into each resulting quotient, until the quotient is smaller than 3. Next, put the final quotient as the first digit. Then go backwards and write the remainders and place them as digits, in order from left to right.

23. D: The rectangular array represents the product of the side lengths of 5 and $(3 + 4)$.

24. C: The original price may be represented by the equation $6{,}375 = x - 0.15x$ or $6{,}375 = 0.85x$. Dividing both sides of the equation by 0.85 gives $x = 7{,}500$.

25. B: The decimal point is 3 places to the right of the first digit, 2. Thus, $2{,}417 = 2.417 \times 10^3$.

Algebra and Functions

26. D: The position of a decelerating car is changing according to a non-constant speed. Thus, the graph will show a curve with a decreasing slope. The slope is decreasing since it represents the velocity, and the velocity is decreasing.

27. D: A vertical line will cross the graph at more than one point. Thus, it is not a function.

28. A: The table shows the y-intercept to be –2. The slope is equal to the ratio of change in y-values to change in corresponding x-values. As each x-value increases by 1, each y-value increases by 2. Thus, the slope is $\frac{2}{1}$, or 2. This graph represents the equation $y = 2x - 2$.

29. A: The value of the 35th term may be found using the formula $a_n = a_1 + (n - 1)d$. Substituting the number of terms for n, the initial value of 1 for a, and the common difference of 2 for d gives: $a_{35} = 1 + (35 - 1)(2)$, which simplifies to $a_{35} = 69$. Now, the value of the 35th term may be substituted into the formula, $S_n = \frac{n(a_1 + a_n)}{2}$, which gives: $S_{50} = \frac{35(1+69)}{2}$, which simplifies to $S_{35} = 1,225$.

30. C: An inverse relationship is represented by an equation in the form $y = \frac{k}{x}$, where k represents some constant of proportionality. The graph of this equation is a hyperbola, symmetric about the y-axis.

31. A: If we divide both terms in the numerator by n^2, the expression reduces to $\frac{1}{n} - \frac{1}{n^2}$. Both $\frac{1}{n}$ and $\frac{1}{n^2}$ converge to 0, so the expression can be written as $0 - 0 = 0$. Thus the limit is 0.

32. C: Using the points $(-6, 1)$ and $(-2, 3)$, the slope may be written as $m = \frac{3-1}{-2-(-6)}$ or $m = \frac{1}{2}$. Substituting the slope of $\frac{1}{2}$ and the x- and y-values from the point $(-6, 1)$ into the slope-intercept form of an equation gives $1 = -6(\frac{1}{2}) + b$, which simplifies to $1 = -3 + b$. Adding 3 to both sides of the equation gives $b = 4$. Thus, the linear equation that includes the data in the table is $y = \frac{1}{2}x + 4$.

33. C: The lines cross at the point with an x-value of –2 and a y-value of –1. Thus, the solution is $(-2, -1)$.

34. C: The constant of proportionality is equal to the slope. Using the points, $(-3, 9)$ and $(0, 0)$, the slope may be written as $\frac{0-9}{0-(-3)}$, which equals –3.

35. B: The graph shows $f(1) = 0$. Since the y-intercept of the parabola is –3, the following equation may be written: $0 = a(1)^2 - 3$, which simplifies to $0 = a - 3$, or $a = 3$. Thus, the graph represents the function $f(x) = 3x^2 - 3$. Evaluating this function for an x-value of 3 gives $f(3) = 3(3)^2 - 3$ or $f(3) = 24$. The average rate of change may be written as $A(x) = \frac{24-0}{3-1}$, which simplifies to $A(x) = 12$.

36. A: The horizontal asymptote is equal to the ratio of the two coefficients of x, or $\frac{2}{-1}$, which equals –2.

37. C: The test point of $(0, 0)$ indicates that shading should occur above both lines. Graph C shows the darker shading above both lines.

38. D: As x goes to positive or negative infinity, only the leading term of a polynomial function of x matters. Therefore, we can ignore the "+2" in the denominator; $\lim_{x\to\infty} \frac{2x^3}{x^2+2} = \lim_{x\to\infty} \frac{2x^3}{x^2} = \lim_{x\to\infty} 2x$. As x goes to positive infinity, $2x$ increases without bound. The expression therefore has no limit.

39. A: As the denominator approaches infinity, the value of the function will get smaller and smaller and converge to 0.

40. D: Since she spends at least $40, the relation of the number of sandwiches to the minimum cost may be written as $8s \geq 40$. Alternatively, the inequality may be written as $40 \leq 8s$.

41. A: The graph of a proportional relationship is a straight line that passes through the origin, or point $(0, 0)$.

42. C: This graph shows a slope of $\frac{1}{2}$, a y-intercept of -2, and the correct shading below the line. Using the test point $(0, 0)$, the equation $0 \leq 0 - 2$ may be written. Since 0 is not less than or equal to -2, the solution is the shaded area below the line, which does not contain the point $(0, 0)$.

43. B: The situation may be modeled by the inequality $2.5x + 6y \leq 30$. Isolating the y-term gives $6y \leq -2.5x + 30$. Solving for y gives $y \leq -\frac{5}{12}x + 5$. Thus, the y-intercept will be 5, the line will be solid, and a test point of $(0, 0)$ indicates the shading should occur below the line.

44. C: An inverse proportional relationship is written in the form $y = \frac{k}{x}$, thus the equation $y = -\frac{7}{x}$ shows that y is inversely proportional to x.

45. A: The graph is a straight line that does not pass through the origin, or $(0, 0)$. Thus, it is linear but not proportional.

46. A: Relation A is the only one in which there is not any x-value that is mapped to more than one y-value. Thus, this relation represents a function.

47. C: The table represents part of a geometric sequence, with a common ratio of 3, so it also represents points of an exponential function.

48. B: The expression $(x + 6)^2$ may be expanded as $x^2 + 12x + 36$. Multiplication of $-2x$ by this expression gives $-2x^3 - 24x^2 - 72x$.

49. B: The limit is simply the quotient of $-4n$ divided by n, or -4.

50. D: The derivative of an equation of the form $y = ax^n$ is equal to $(n \times a)x^{n-1}$. So the derivative of $y = 3x^5$ is equal to $(5 \times 3)x^{5-1}$ or $15x^4$.

51. B: The limit of the expression $\frac{7x^2}{x^2}$, is 7, so the limit of the entire function is $12 - 7 = 5$. The function converges.

52. A: The horizontal asymptote is equal to the ratio of the coefficient of $-x$ to the coefficient of $4x$, or $-\frac{1}{4}$.

53. C: The inequality will be less than or equal to, since she may spend $25 or less on her purchase.

54. C: The slope is equal to 12, since each ticket costs $12. The y-intercept is represented by the constant fee of $8. Substituting 12 for m and 8 for b into the equation $y = mx + b$ gives $y = 12x + 8$.

55. A: Graph B shows the correct y-intercept of 2 and graph C shows the correct slope of $-\frac{1}{2}$, but only graph A shows both the correct slope and y-intercept. Using the points $(0, 2)$ and $4, 0)$, the slope of graph A may be written as $m = \frac{0-2}{4-0}$, which simplifies to $m = -\frac{1}{2}$.

Mometrix

56. B: The points in the table represent a symmetrical curve mirrored across the y-axis. This is a parabola, or quadratic equation.

57. B: The product of $(x + 3)(3x - 6)$ equals $3x^2 - 6x + 9x - 18$, which simplifies to $3x^2 + 3x - 18$.

58. A: The sum of –8 and the product of each term number and 7 equals the term value. For example, for term number 4, the value is equal to $7(4) - 8$, or 20.

59. C: The ratio between successive terms is constant (3), so this is a geometric series. A geometric sequence is represented by an exponential function.

60. C: This situation may be modeled by an arithmetic sequence, with a common difference of 5 and initial value of 15. Substituting the common difference and initial value into the formula, $a_n = a_1 + (n - 1)d$, gives $a_n = 15 + (n - 1)5$, which simplifies to $a_n = 5n + 10$.

61. B: A graph of the function shows the positive x-intercept to occur at approximately $(2.3, 0)$. Thus, the ball will reach the ground after approximately 2.3 seconds.

62. A: This graph is shifted 2 units to the left and 3 units down from that of the parent function, $y = x^2$.

63. A: The sign of the constant, inside the squared term, is positive for a shift to the left and negative for a shift to the right. Thus, a movement of 4 units right is indicated by the expression $y = (x - 4)^2$. A shift of 6 units down is indicated by subtraction of 6 units from the squared term.

64. C: The derivative of an equation of the form $y = x^n$ is equal to $n \times x^{n-1}$. So the derivative of $g(x) = x^{2yz}$ is equal to $2yz \times x^{2yz-1}$.

65. B: The slope of the graphed line is $-\frac{1}{3}$. A line parallel to this one will also have a slope of $-\frac{1}{3}$. Substituting the slope and the x- and y-values from the point $(-2, 1)$, into the slope-intercept form of an equation gives: $1 = -\frac{1}{3}(-2) + b$, which simplifies to $1 = \frac{2}{3} + b$. Subtracting $\frac{2}{3}$ from both sides of the equation gives $b = \frac{1}{3}$. So the equation of a line parallel to this one and passing through the point $(-2, 1)$ is $y = -\frac{1}{3}x + \frac{1}{3}$.

66. D: The slope of the graphed line is $\frac{1}{2}$. A line perpendicular to this one will have a slope of –2. Substituting the slope and the x- and y-values from the point $(1, -2)$, into the slope-intercept form of an equation gives: $-2 = -2(1) + b$, which simplifies to $-2 = -2 + b$. Adding 2 to each side of the equation gives $b = 0$. So the equation of a line perpendicular to this one and passing through the point $(1, -2)$ is $y = -2x$.

67. D: The sequence $\frac{1}{3}, \frac{1}{9}, \frac{1}{27}, \frac{1}{81}, \ldots$, may be used to represent the situation. Substituting the initial value of $\frac{1}{3}$ and common ratio of $\frac{1}{3}$ into the formula $S = \frac{a}{1-r}$ gives $= \frac{\frac{1}{3}}{1-\frac{1}{3}}$, which simplifies to $S = \frac{\frac{1}{3}}{\frac{2}{3}}$ or $S = \frac{1}{2}$.

68. D: The situation may be modeled with the equation $\frac{1}{15} + \frac{1}{20} = \frac{1}{t}$, which simplifies to $\frac{7}{60} = \frac{1}{t}$. Thus, $t = \frac{60}{7}$. If working together, it will take them approximately 8.6 minutes to finish the dishes.

46

69. C: The situation may be modeled by the system $\begin{array}{l}6x + 2y = 7.20\\15x + y = 12.60\end{array}$. Multiplying the bottom equation by –2 gives $\begin{array}{l}6x + 2y = 7.20\\-30x - 2y = -25.20\end{array}$. Addition of the two equations gives $-24x = -18$ or $x = 0.75$. Thus, one pen costs \$0.75. We can plug this value back into the second equation to obtain $15(0.75) + y = 12.60$, or $11.25 + y = 12.60$. Subtracting 11.25 from each side yields $y = 1.35$, so one notebook costs \$1.35.

70. C: Evaluation of the expression for an x-value of $\frac{1}{2}$ gives: $\left(8(\frac{1}{2})^2 - 6(\frac{1}{2}) + 3\right)$, which equals 2.

71. C: The situation may be modeled by the following system of inequalities: $\begin{array}{l}3x + 5y \le 60\\x + y \ge 15\end{array}$. A test point of $(0, 0)$ indicates shading should occur below the line for the top equation and above the line for the bottom equation. The overlapped shading occurs in the lower right portion between the lines. Thus, graph C represents the correct combinations of items that Myles may purchase, given his budget.

72. C: Substituting –1 for each x-value gives $f(-1) = \frac{(-1)^3 + 3(-1) + 2}{2(-1)}$, which simplifies to $f(-1) = 1$.

73. C: The sum of an infinite geometric series may be modeled by the formula $S = \frac{a}{1-r}$, where a represents the initial value and r represents the common ratio. Substituting the initial value of 5 and common ratio of $\frac{3}{5}$ into the formula gives $= \frac{5}{1-\frac{3}{5}}$, which simplifies to $S = \frac{5}{\frac{2}{5}}$ or $\frac{25}{2}$. This can be written as 12.5.

74. B: This situation may be modeled by a geometric sequence, with a common ratio of 3 and initial value of 2. Substituting the common ratio and initial value into the formula $a_n = a_1 \times r^{n-1}$ gives $a_n = 2 \times 3^{n-1}$.

75. C: On a graph, the lines intersect at the point, $(3, -6)$. Thus, $(3, -6)$ is the solution to the system of linear equations.

Measurement and Geometry

76. D: The surface area of a sphere may be calculated using the formula $SA = 4\pi r^2$. Substituting 0.8 for r gives $SA = 4\pi(0.8)^2$, which simplifies to $SA \approx 8.04$. So the surface area of the ball is approximately 8.04 square feet. There are twelve inches in a foot, so there are $12^2 = 144$ square inches in a square foot. In order to convert this measurement to square inches, then, the following proportion may be written and solved for x: $\frac{144}{1} = \frac{x}{8.04}$. So $x \approx 1{,}157.76$. It would take approximately 1,157.76 square feet of wrapping paper to wrap the ball.

77. B: The net of a square pyramid has a square base and four triangular faces. So only B can be folded into a triangular prism.

78. A: The slope may be written as $m = \frac{5 - (-1)}{-4 - 3}$, which simplifies to $m = -\frac{6}{7}$.

79. A: A reflection across the y-axis results in a triangle with vertices at $(-3, 3)$, $(-3, 7.5)$, and $(-6, 3)$. A rotation of 90 degrees is denoted by the following: $(a, b) \to (-b, a)$. Thus, rotating the reflected triangle by 90 degrees will result in a figure with vertices at $(-3, -3)$, $(-7.5, -3)$, and $(-3, -6)$. The transformed triangle indeed has these coordinates as its vertices.

80. B: The surface area of a rectangular prism may be calculated using the formula $SA = 2lw + 2wh + 2hl$. Substituting the dimensions of 12 feet, 9 feet, and 10 feet gives $SA = 2(12)(10) + 2(10)(9) + 2(9)(12)$. Thus, the surface area is 636 square feet.

81. C: The measure of the angle formed by the chord and the tangent is equal to one-half of the measure of the intercepted arc. Since the measure of the angle is 112°, the measure of the intercepted arc may be found by writing $112° = \frac{1}{2}x$. Dividing both sides of the equation by $\frac{1}{2}$ gives $x = 224°$. The measure of the intercepted arc may also be found by multiplying 112° by 2. Thus, the value of x is 224°.

82. A: The cross-section of a triangular prism will never be a circle.

83. D: The figure is a hexagon, which can be divided into two equal trapezoids. The area of a trapezoid may be calculated using the formula $A = \frac{1}{2}(b_1 + b_2)h$. Thus, the area of the trapezoid is represented as $A = \frac{1}{2}(7 + 3)(3)$, which simplifies to $A = 15$. We double this for the area of the hexagon. Thus, the total area is 30 square units.

84. B: The volume of a prism may be calculated using the formula $V = Bh$, where B represents the area of the base and h represents the height of the prism. The area of each triangular base is represented by $A = \frac{1}{2}(7.5)(10)$. So the area of each base is equal to 37.5 square centimeters. Substituting 37.5 for the area of the base and 12 for the height of the prism gives $V = (37.5)(12)$ or $V = 450$. The volume of the prism is 450 cm³.

85. B: The volume of a pyramid may be calculated using the formula $V = \frac{1}{3}Bh$, where B represents the area of the base and h represents the height. Since the base is a square, the area of the base is equal to 3.5^2, or 12.25 square inches. Substituting 12.25 for B and 6 for h gives $V = \frac{1}{3}(12.25)(6)$, which simplifies to $V = 24.5$.

86. C: The distance may be calculated using the distance formula, $d = \sqrt{(x_2 - x_1)^2 + (y_2 - y_1)^2}$. Substituting the given coordinates, the following equation may be written:

$$d = \sqrt{\left(-4 - (8)\right)^2 + (8 - -3)^2}$$
$$d = \sqrt{265}$$

87. C: The Pythagorean Theorem may be used to find the diagonal distance from the top of the tree to the base of the shadow. The following equation may be written and solved for c: $12^2 + 9.8^2 = c^2$. Thus, $c \approx 15.5$. The distance is approximately 15.5 ft.

88. C: The following proportion may be written and solved for x: $\frac{12^2}{1} = \frac{x}{17.85}$. So $x = 144(17.85) = 2,570.4$. Thus, 17.85 square feet is approximately equal to 2,570 square inches.

89. A: The alternate interior angles have congruent angle measures, each measuring 142°. According to the Alternate Interior Angles Converse Theorem, two lines are parallel if a transversal, intersecting the lines, forms congruent alternate interior angles.

90. B: The amount Zel drinks may be written as $\frac{1}{8} \times \frac{20}{3}$, which equals $\frac{20}{24}$ or $\frac{5}{6}$. Thus, she drinks $\frac{5}{6}$ fluid ounces of juice.

91. D: The perimeter of the triangle is equal to the sum of the side lengths. The lengths of the two legs are 9 and 12 units. The length of the hypotenuse may be represented as $d = \sqrt{(9)^2 + (12)^2}$, which simplifies to $d = 15$. Thus, the perimeter is equal to $9 + 12 + 15$, which is 36 units. Since each unit represents 3.5 miles, the total distance of the path is equal to the product of 15 and 3.5, or 126 miles.

92. A: The volume of a cylinder may be calculated using the formula $V = \pi r^2 h$, where r represents the radius and h represents the height. Substituting 2 for r (half of the diameter) and 4.5 for h gives $V = \pi(2)^2(4.5)$, which simplifies to $V \approx 56.5$.

93. D: The triangle is a 45-45-90 right triangle. Thus, if each leg is represented by x, the hypotenuse is represented by $x\sqrt{2}$. Thus, the hypotenuse is equal to $12\sqrt{2}$ in.

94. C: The measure of the inscribed angle is half of the measure of the intercepted arc. Since the inscribed angle measures 62°, the intercepted arc is equal to (62°)(2) or 124°.

95. C: The relationship between number of faces, edges, and vertices is represented by Euler's Formula, $E = F + V - 2$. Substituting 12 for E and 8 for V gives: $12 = F + 8 - 2$, which simplifies to $12 = F + 6$. Thus, $F = 6$.

96. A: The area of the rectangle is equal to 10(20), or 200 square centimeters. The area of the circle is equal to $\pi(5)^2$, or approximately 78.5 square centimeters. The area of the shaded region is equal to the difference of the area of the rectangle and the area of the circle, or 200 cm² − 78.5 cm², which equals 121.5 cm². So the area of the shaded region is about 122 cm².

97. D: The triangle was dilated. Dilating an image produces a new image with the same proportions but different dimensions.

98. D: The following equation may be written and solved for x: $\sin 62° = \frac{x}{10}$. Multiplying both sides of the equation by 10 gives: $10 \times \sin 62° = x$, or $x \approx 8.8$.

99. A: The following proportion may be written and solved for x: $\frac{5,280}{1} = \frac{4,900}{x}$. Thus, $x \approx 0.93$.

100. B: The volume of a sphere may be calculated using the formula $V = \frac{4}{3}\pi r^3$, where r represents the radius. Substituting 2.75 for r gives $V = \frac{4}{3}\pi(2.75)^3$, which simplifies to $V \approx 87.1$.

101. D: The following proportion may be written and solved for x: $\frac{20}{15} = \frac{5}{x}$. Solving for x gives $x = 3.75$. Thus, the shadow cast by the person is 3.75 feet in length.

102. B: The perimeter is equal to the sum of the lengths of the two bases, 6 and 2 units, and the diagonal distances of the other two sides. Using the distance formula, each side length may be represented as $d = \sqrt{20} = 2\sqrt{5}$. Thus, the sum of the two sides is equal to $2\sqrt{20}$, or $4\sqrt{5}$. The whole perimeter is equal to $8 + 4\sqrt{5}$.

103. A: Equilateral triangles and squares may tessellate a plane. Each triangle may be attached to each side of a square, leaving no gaps in the plane.

104. C: The measure of an angle formed by intersecting chords inside a circle is equal to one-half of the sum of the measures of the intercepted arcs. Thus, $x = \frac{1}{2}(88° + 62°)$, or 75°.

105. A: ∠n and ∠s are corresponding angles. Thus, they are congruent.

106. C: The larger triangle has a base length of 6 units and a height of 6 units. The smaller triangle has a base length of 3 units and a height of 3 units. Thus, the dimensions of the larger triangle were multiplied by a scale factor of $\frac{1}{2}$.

107. B: The midpoint may be calculated by using the formula $m = \left(\frac{x_1+x_2}{2}, \frac{y_1+y_2}{2}\right)$. Thus, the midpoint of the line segment shown may be written as $m = \left(\frac{-5+7}{2}, \frac{-3+5}{2}\right)$, which simplifies to $m = (1,1)$.

108. B: Since the figures are similar, the following proportion may be written and solved for x: $\frac{5}{7.5} = \frac{12}{x}$. Thus, $x = \frac{90}{5}$ or 18.

109. C: Two of the sides, plus the angle between them, are congruent to the corresponding sides and angle of the other triangle. Thus, the SAS (Side-Angle-Side) Theorem may be used to prove the congruence of the triangles.

110. A: The vertical line of symmetry is represented by an equation of the form $x = a$. The horizontal line of symmetry is represented by an equation of the form $y = a$. One line of symmetry occurs at $x = -2$. The other line of symmetry occurs at $y = 4$.

111. D: The two triangles are similar because all three sides of triangle MNP are greater than the corresponding sides of triangle QNR by a factor of 1.5. So the two triangles are similar according to the SSS (Side-Side-Side) Similarity Postulate.

112. D: When two parallel lines are cut by a transversal, corresponding angles are congruent.

Statistics, Probability, and Discrete Mathematics

113. B: Both p and q must be true in order for the intersection to be true. So, I is incorrect but II and III are correct.

114. C: The theoretical probability is $\frac{1}{2}$, and $\frac{1}{2}(250) = 125$.

115. A: A tautology will show all true values in a truth table column. Look at the table below:

p	q	$p \wedge q$	$(p \wedge q) \rightarrow p$
T	T	F	T
T	F	F	T
F	T	T	T
F	F	T	T

Only the statement $(p \wedge q) \rightarrow p$ shows all T's in the column.

116. D: The intersection of the two sets is empty, denoted by the symbol, ∅. There are not any elements common to both sets.

117. B: The number of ways the letters can be arranged may be represented as $\frac{5!}{2!1!1!1!}$, which equals 60.

118. B: Data sets A and C are asymmetrical: data set A is skewed toward lower values, and data set C is skewed toward higher values. This makes the mean a poor measure of center. Data set D is mostly symmetrical, but has a small outlier. The mean is very sensitive to outliers, and is not an appropriate measure of center for data sets that include them. Data set B is roughly symmetrical and has no outliers; the mean would be an appropriate measure of center here.

119. D: The number of outcomes in the event is 4 (rolling a 3, 4, 5, or 6), and the sample space is 6 (numbers 1–6). Thus, the probability may be written as $\frac{4}{6}$, which simplifies to $\frac{2}{3}$.

120. C: A z-score may be calculated using the formula $z = \frac{X-\mu}{\sigma}$. Substituting the score of 92, class average of 86, and class standard deviation of 2.5 into the formula gives: $z = \frac{92-86}{2.5}$, which simplifies to $z = 2.4$. Thus, the student's score is 2.4 standard deviations above the mean.

121. B: The median of the lower half of the scores is 7. The median of the upper half of the scores is 18. The interquartile range is equal to the difference in the first and third quartiles. Thus, the interquartile range is 11.

122. D: Choosing either the 50 youngest or 50 oldest people in a group is likely to increase sampling error, since randomization was not employed. The other described techniques utilize random sampling or other methods of decreasing sampling error.

123. A: The z-score is written as $z = \frac{70-85}{5}$, which simplifies to $z = -3$. A z-score with an absolute value of 3 shows a mean to z area of 0.4987. Subtracting this area from 0.5 gives 0.0013, or 0.13%.

124. A: Two z-scores should be calculated, one for each student's score. The first z-score may be written as $z = \frac{71-81}{10}$, which simplifies to $z = -1$. The second z-score may be written as $z = \frac{86-81}{10}$, which simplifies to $z = 0.5$. The percentage of students scoring between these two scores is equal to the sum of the two mean to z areas. A z-score with an absolute value of 1 shows a mean to z area of 0.3413. A z-score of 0.5 shows a mean to z area of 0.1915. The sum of these two areas is 0.5328, or 53.28%.

125. D: A z-score of 2.5 has a mean to z area of 0.4938, or 49.38%. Twice this percentage is about 99%.

126. B: The points may be entered into a graphing calculator or Excel spreadsheet to find the least-squares regression line. This line is approximately $y = 1.67x + 1.74$. Substituting 15 for x gives $y = 1.67(15) + 1.74$, or $y = 26.79$. Thus, $27 is a good estimate for the profit received for selling 15 items. If a line of best fit is predicted visually, the slope between points near that line is approximately $1\frac{3}{4}$, and the line passes near the origin. This gives an estimate of $27.75, which is closer to $27 than any of the other choices.

127. B: Since there are 8 numerals, the answer is equal to 8!, or 40,320.

128. C: The series is an infinite geometric series. The sum may be calculated using the formula $S = \frac{a}{1-r}$, where a represents the value of the first term and r represents the common ratio. Substituting 1 for a and $\frac{1}{3}$ for r gives $S = \frac{1}{1-\frac{1}{3}}$ or $1\frac{1}{2}$.

129. C: Only when both p and q are false is the union of p and q false. So, both I and II are correct.

130. B: Since they are not mutually exclusive events, the probability may be written as $P(6 \text{ or } E) = P(6) + P(E) - P(6 \text{ and } E)$. Substituting the probability of each event gives $(6 \text{ or } E) = \frac{1}{6} + \frac{1}{2} - \frac{1}{6}$, or $\frac{1}{2}$.

131. D: This is a counting problem. The possible number of outfits is equal to the product of the possibilities for each category. The product of 4, 6, and 5 is 120. Thus, there are 120 outfits that she may create.

132. C: A t-test should be used. A t-score may be calculated using the formula $t = \frac{\bar{X} - \mu}{\frac{s}{\sqrt{n}}}$. Substituting the sample mean, population mean, sample standard deviation, and sample size into the formula gives $t = \frac{26.5 - 27}{\frac{1.5}{\sqrt{25}}}$ which simplifies to $t \approx 1.67$. For degrees of freedom of 24, the p-value is approximately 0.054. Thus, there is not a significant difference between what the company claimed to be the average hourly wage and what the actual sample average showed. The claim is likely true, as evidenced by a p-value greater than 0.05.

133. B: $A \cup B$ means "A union B," or all of the elements in either of the two sets. "A union B" represents "A or B," that is, an element is in the union of A and B if it is in A *or* it is in B. The elements in sets A and B are −3, −1, 0, 1, 2, 3, 4, 6, and 9.

134. D: The z-score is written as $z = \frac{72 - 84}{8}$, which simplifies to $z = -1.5$. A z-score with an absolute value of 1.5 shows a mean to z area of 0.4332. Adding 0.5 to this area gives 0.9332, or 93.32%.

135. C: The number in the sample space is equal to the number of possible outcomes for one coin toss, 2, raised to the power of the number of coin tosses, or 5. $2^5 = 32$.

136. C: A t-test should be used. A t-score may be calculated using the formula $t = \frac{\bar{X} - \mu}{\frac{s}{\sqrt{n}}}$. Substituting the sample mean, population mean, sample standard deviation, and sample size into the formula gives $t = \frac{146 - 150}{\frac{3}{\sqrt{25}}}$, which simplifies to $t \approx -6.67$. For degrees of freedom of 24, any t-value greater than 3.75 will have a p-value less than 0.001. Thus, there is a significant difference between what the manufacturer claims and the actual amount included in each box. The claim is likely false, due to a p-value less than 0.01.

137. C: The standard deviation is equal to the square root of the ratio of the sum of the squares of the deviation of each score from the mean to the square root of the difference of n and 1. The mean of the data set is 13.5. The deviations are −5.5, −3.5, −2.5, −0.5, −0.5, 2.5, 3.5, and 6.5. The sum of the squares of the deviations may be written as:

$$30.25 + 12.25 + 6.25 + 0.25 + 0.25 + 6.25 + 12.25 + 42.25 = 110$$

Division of this sum by $n - 1 = 7$ gives 15.71. The square root of this quotient is approximately 4.0.

138. B: $A \cap B$ means "A intersect B," or the elements that are common to both sets. "A intersect B" represents "A and B," that is, an element is in the intersection of A and B if it is in A *and* it is in B. The elements 1, 2, and 4 are common to both sets.

139. D: In a positively skewed distribution, the median is closer to the first quartile than the third.

Mometrix

140. A: The probability may be written as $P(N \text{ and } H) = P(N) \times P(H)$. Substituting the probability of each event gives $(N \text{ and } H) = \frac{1}{3} \times \frac{1}{2}$, which simplifies to $\frac{1}{6}$.

141. C: A Venn diagram may be drawn to assist in finding the answer.

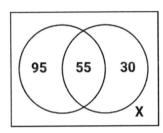

Since the set contains 225 total people, the solution is equal to $225 - (95 + 55 + 30)$ or 45 people

142. D: The probability may be written as $P(B \text{ or } CS) = P(B) + P(CS) - P(B \text{ and } CS)$. Substituting the probabilities, the following may be written: $P(B \text{ or } CS) = \frac{1233}{1810} + \frac{971}{1810} - \frac{642}{1810}$, which simplifies to $P(B \text{ or } CS) = \frac{1562}{1810}$ or approximately 85%.

143. C: A z-test may be used, since the population standard deviation is known. A z-score may be calculated using the formula $z = \frac{\bar{X} - \mu}{\frac{\sigma}{\sqrt{n}}}$. Substituting the sample mean, population mean, population standard deviation, and sample size into the formula gives $z = \frac{16.1 - 16}{\frac{0.2}{\sqrt{30}}}$, which simplifies to $z \approx 2.74$.

The p-value is approximately 0.006, which is less than 0.05. Thus, there does appear to be a significant difference between what the manufacturer claims and the actual number of ounces found in each container. The claim is likely not true, due to a p-value less than 0.05.

144. C: If the statement is written in the form $p \rightarrow q$, then the converse is represented as $q \rightarrow p$. Thus, the converse should read, "If Joe buys a donut, it is Saturday."

145. C: Since they are not mutually exclusive events, the probability may be written as $P(N \text{ or } T) = P(N) + P(T) - P(N \text{ and } T)$. Because the events are independent, $P(N \text{ and } T) = P(N) \times P(T)$. Substituting the probability of each event gives $(N \text{ or } T) = \frac{1}{2} + \frac{1}{2} - \left(\frac{1}{2} \times \frac{1}{2}\right)$, or $\frac{3}{4}$.

146. C: A conditional statement $p \rightarrow q$ and its contrapositive $\neg q \rightarrow \neg p$ are logically equivalent because of the identical values in a truth table. See below.

p	q	$\neg p$	$\neg q$	$p \rightarrow q$	$\neg q \rightarrow \neg p$
T	T	F	F	T	T
T	F	F	T	F	F
F	T	T	F	T	T
F	F	T	T	T	T

147. B: If the statement is written in the form $p \rightarrow q$, then the contrapositive is represented as $\neg q \rightarrow \neg p$. Thus, the contrapositive should read, "If Bryan does not have an allergic reaction, he does not eat peanuts."

53

148. D: A two-sample t-test should be used. Entering the sample mean, sample standard deviation, and sample size of each group into a graphing calculator reveals a p-value that is less than 0.05, so a significant difference between the groups may be declared.

149. D: This situation describes a permutation, since order matters. The formula for calculating a combination is $P(n, r) = \frac{n!}{(n-r)!}$. This situation may be represented as $P(7,4) = \frac{7!}{(7-4)!}$, which equals 840.

150. A: The ends of Dataset A are farther apart (from 3 to 17 instead of 3 to 15), indicating a larger range. The horizontal line in the middle of a boxplot represents the median, so Dataset A also has a larger median (9.5 instead of 9).

Constructed Response

1. A. First, according to the problem, c is the value of the computer after its initial depreciation. The laptop's value drops by 10%, so:

$$c = \$1,850 - (0.1) \times (\$1,850) = \$1,665$$

Using this value for c and substituting it in, the value formula then becomes:

$$y = \$1,665 - (0.03) \times (\$1,665) \times (x)$$

Finally, since 1 year is 12 months, solve for y when $x = 12$:

$$y = \$1,665 - (0.03) \times (\$1,665) \times (12)$$
$$y = \$1,665 - \$599.40$$
$$y = \$1,065.60$$

1. B. The graph of y will be linear since x is raised to the first power. Reordering the function to the $y = mx + b$ format, the y-intercept and slope are readily identifiable:

$$y = \$1,665 - \left(\frac{\$49.95}{month}\right) \times (x)$$
$$y = -\left(\frac{\$49.95}{month}\right) \times (x) + \$1,665$$

Thus, the slope is $-\$49.95$ per month and the y-intercept is $\$1,665$. Plotting this function looks like the following.

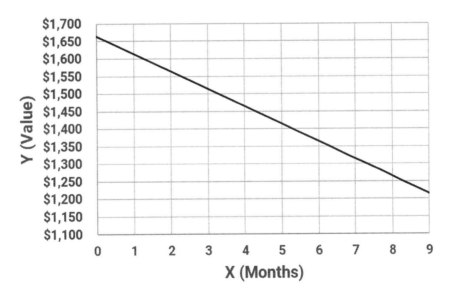

1. C. Using the axis values, it is readily apparent that the value function approaches $1,500 a little after 3 months. We can estimate that it is about 3.5 months from the graph.

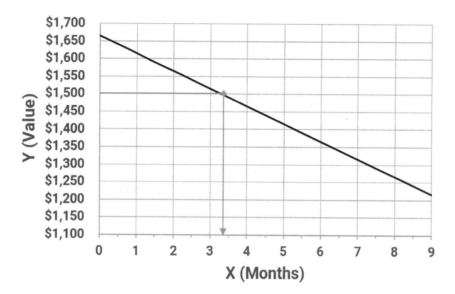

1. D. The way to use the function to find when the value is $1,500 is to substitute it in for y and solve for x:

$$\$1,500 = \$1,665 - \left(\frac{\$49.95}{month}\right) \times (x)$$

$$-\$165 = -\left(\frac{\$49.95}{month}\right) \times (x)$$

$$\frac{-\$165}{-\left(\frac{\$49.95}{month}\right)} = x$$

$$x = 3.303 \text{ months}$$

After rounding to the tenths place: $x = 3.3$ months

2. A. The vendor area is in the 4 squares only. We can find the area of one square and multiply by 4 to get the total vendor area. Since each side is 10 ft:

$$A_{vendors} = 4 \times s^2$$
$$A_{vendors} = 4 \times (10 \text{ ft})^2$$
$$A_{vendors} = 400 \text{ ft}^2$$

2. B. The first step in finding the percent walkway area is to find the area of the circle, which can be written as πr^2. Since the diameter is 30 ft, we know that the radius is 15 ft:

$$A = \pi \times (15 \text{ ft})^2$$
$$A \cong 706.5 \text{ ft}^2$$

Next, we can use the information from part A to find the area of the circle minus the area of the vendor booths to give us the total walking area. If the total area of the circle is approximately

706.5 ft^2 and the area of the vendor booths is 400 ft^2, then the area within the circle but around the booths is $706.5 - 400 \cong 306.5$ ft^2.

The percent walkway area is found by:

$$walkway\% = \frac{A_{walkway}}{A_{triangle}} \times 100\%$$
$$walkway\% \cong \frac{306.5 \text{ ft}^2}{706.5 \text{ ft}^2} \times 100\%$$
$$walkway\% \cong 43.4\%$$

2. C. It can be assumed that a point has an equal chance of being anywhere in the area of the circle. Thus, the probability it will land in a vendor area is given by:

$$P_{vendor} = \frac{A_{vendor}}{A_{circle}} \cong \frac{400 \text{ ft}^2}{706.5 \text{ ft}^2} \cong 0.566$$

3. A. The median of a list of values is the centermost value of an ordered list. If the ordered list has an even number of members, then the median is the average of the two centermost values. The two center values in this list are 63 and 64, so we add them and divide by 2 to find the median. The range of a list is the difference of the highest value and the lowest value. Thus, for this problem, the median is $\frac{63+64}{2} = 63.5$ lb and the range is $83 - 51 = 32$ lb.

3. B. The mean of a list of values is the sum of all the members of the list divided by the number of members in the list:

$$mean = \frac{51 + 2(54) + 56 + 59 + 60 + 62 + 63 + 2(64) + 67 + 2(69) + 73 + 76 + 83}{16}$$
$$mean = 64 \text{ lb}$$

3. C. The stem and leaf plot would look like this:

```
5 | 1  4  4  6  9
6 | 0  2  3  4  4  7  9  9
7 | 3  6
8 | 3
```

Practice Test #2

Number Sense and Operations

1. Which of the following correctly represents the expanded form of 0.158?

    a. $1 \times \frac{1}{10^0} + 5 \times \frac{1}{10^1} + 8 \times \frac{1}{10^2}$

    b. $1 \times \frac{1}{10^1} + 5 \times \frac{1}{10^2} + 8 \times \frac{1}{10^3}$

    c. $1 \times \frac{1}{10^3} + 5 \times \frac{1}{10^2} + 8 \times \frac{1}{10^1}$

    d. $1 \times \frac{1}{10^2} + 5 \times \frac{1}{10^3} + 8 \times \frac{1}{10^4}$

2. Which of the following equations may be used to convert $0.\overline{8}$ to a fraction?

    a. $9x = 80$
    b. $90x = 8$
    c. $9x = 8$
    d. $99x = 80$

3. Zac purchases school supplies on a 30% off sale. His cost, after taxes, is $97.78. If the tax rate is 8.5%, what was the original price of the school supplies?

    a. $119.78
    b. $122.01
    c. $125.79
    d. $128.74

4. Which of the following is closed under the operation of multiplication?

    a. whole numbers
    b. negative integers
    c. irrational numbers
    d. none of the above is closed

5. Which expression is represented by the diagram below?

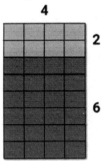

    a. $4 \times (2 + 6)$
    b. $4 \times (2 \times 6)$
    c. $4 + (2 \times 6)$
    d. $4 + (2 + 6)$

58

6. Which of the following statements is true?

   a. The set of whole numbers is a subset of the set of rational numbers.
   b. The set of integers is a subset of the set of whole numbers.
   c. The set of rational numbers is a subset of the set of whole numbers.
   d. The set of whole numbers is a subset of the set of natural numbers.

7. In the base-4 number system, what is the sum of 320 and 1233?

   a. 1543
   b. 2103
   c. 2203
   d. 2213

8. Mario makes an offer of $158,400 on a home. This is a markdown of 12% from the asking price. What was the asking price?

   a. $175,000
   b. $175,550
   c. $178,500
   d. $180,000

9. $p|q$ if

   a. $\frac{p}{q} = 6$
   b. $\frac{q}{p} = 6$
   c. $pq = 6$
   d. $p + q = 6$

10. For any natural numbers, a, b, and c, assume $a < b < c$. Which of the following statements is *not* necessarily true?

   a. $a < c$
   b. $a + b < b + c$
   c. $ab < bc$
   d. $ab < c$

11. Javier finds a laptop on sale for $450. If it had been marked down 40%, what was the original cost?

   a. $800
   b. $750
   c. $650
   d. $600

12. Which of the following represents 47,800?

   a. 4.78×10^{-4}
   b. 4.78×10^{-3}
   c. 4.78×10^{3}
   d. 4.78×10^{4}

13. Which of the following represents 129 in the base-4 system?

    a. 2001
    b. 2301
    c. 10,201
    d. 10,321

14. Which of the following correctly compares the sets of whole numbers and counting numbers?

    a. The sets of whole and counting numbers are equal.
    b. The sets of whole and counting numbers are disjoint.
    c. The set of whole numbers is a subset of the set of counting numbers.
    d. The set of counting numbers is a subset of the set of whole numbers.

15. Which of the following statements is true?

    a. A number is divisible by 8 if the number is divisible by both 2 and 4.
    b. A number is divisible by 6 if the sum of all digits is divisible by 9.
    c. A number is divisible by 4 if the last two digits together are divisible by 4.
    d. A number is divisible by 3 if the sum of the last two digits is divisible by 3.

16. Yu is paid every 2 weeks and sets aside $60 from every paycheck to save for a car. How much does he have in his car fund after a year (count as 52 weeks)?

    a. $1,560
    b. $1,525
    c. $1,490
    d. $1,450

17. Kyra sets aside $\frac{1}{3}$ of her income to pay rent and utilities at her apartment. If the monthly cost of rent and utilities is $1,050, what is her monthly salary?

    a. $3,150
    b. $3,225
    c. $3,750
    d. $4,050

18. Which of the following illustrates the commutative property of multiplication?

    a. The product of a and b is ab.
    b. The product of a and 0 is 0.
    c. The product of a and $-a$ is $-a^2$.
    d. The product of a and b is the same as the product of b and a.

19. Maria uses the pie chart below to represent the allocation of her time on an average 24-hour school day.

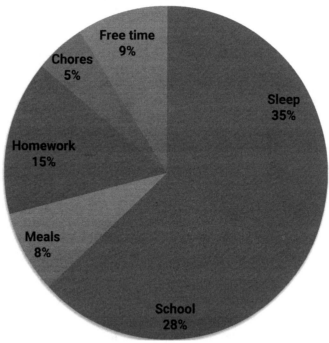

Which of the following statements is true?

   a. The amount of time she spends on sleep is less than 8 hours per night.
   b. The amount of time she spends on chores and free time is approximately 4 hours per day.
   c. The amount of time she spends on meals and homework is more than 5 hours per day.
   d. The amount of time she spends on school is more than 7 hours per day.

20. The table below shows Marc's electricity bill during the summer and autumn months.

Month	Electricity bill
June	$143.79
July	$156.82
August	$160.91
September	$149.28
October	$127.56
November	$138.20

What percentage of Marc's total electricity costs were incurred during the month of October?

   a. 13.5%
   b. 14.6%
   c. 15.9%
   d. 17.2%

21. Which of the following accurately describes the set of rational numbers?

   a. the set of whole numbers
   b. the set of integers plus the roots of positive numbers
   c. the set of numbers that may be written as the ratio of $\frac{a}{b}$, where $b \neq 0$
   d. the set of counting numbers, zero, and the negations of the counting numbers

22. Danielle pays a fee of 0.1% of her paycheck for direct deposit into her bank account. If her monthly paycheck is $3,200, what will her fee be each month?

    a. $0.32
    b. $3.20
    c. $32
    d. $320

23. Which of the following is an irrational number?

    a. $0.\overline{5}$
    b. e^3
    c. $\frac{41}{3}$
    d. $\sqrt{3}^2$

24. Which of the following sets is *not* closed under division?

    a. integers minus zero
    b. real numbers minus zero
    c. rational numbers minus zero
    d. all of the above are closed

25. Eloisa's monthly car payment is $400. She is trading her car in for a newer model with a monthly payment of $525. What is the percent increase in her monthly payment?

    a. 25%
    b. 31.25%
    c. 35%
    d. 42.75%

Algebra and Functions

26. The initial term of a sequence is 7. Each term in the sequence is $\frac{8}{9}$ the amount of the previous term. What is the sum of the terms, as n approaches infinity?

    a. 8

    b. 28.25

    c. 56

    d. 63

27. Jamal is placing an order for ink cartridges and reams of paper. Each ink cartridge costs $7.50. Each ream of paper costs $3. He intends to spend less than $45. Which of the following graphs represents the possible combinations of paper and ink that he may purchase, if the x-axis represents ink cartridges and the y-axis represents reams of paper?

    a. 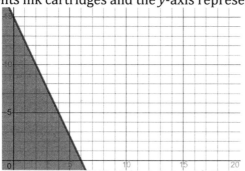   c.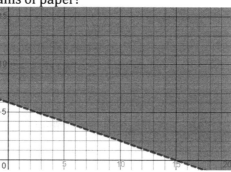

    b. 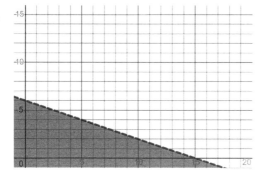   d.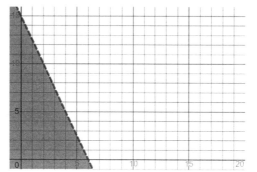

28. What is $\lim\limits_{x \to -4} \left(2x^3 - \frac{1}{2}x^2 - 1\right)$?

    a. -137

    b. -121

    c. 4

    d. 119

29. $f(x) = \frac{3x-5}{2x}$. What is the equation of the horizontal asymptote?

    a. $y = -\frac{5}{2}$

    b. $y = \frac{1}{2}$

    c. $y = 0$

    d. $y = \frac{3}{2}$

30. Which of the following represents a function?

    a. $\{(2, 9), (3, 5), (6, 8), (-1, -6), (3, -2)\}$
    b. $\{(8, 8), (7, 9), (2, 1), (8, 3), (3, 6)\}$
    c. $\{(-4, 6), (2, 4), (-4, -2), (3, 5), (9, 2)\}$
    d. $\{(2, 6), (6, 5), (5, 9), (1, 0), (-3, 1)\}$

31. Which of the following functions has a limit of 0?

    a. $f(x) = 6x^2 - 6$
    b. $f(x) = \frac{4x}{x}$
    c. $f(x) = \frac{3}{x+3}$
    d. $f(x) = \frac{x+1}{x}$

32. Which of the following formulas may be used to represent the sequence 8, 12, 16, 20, 24, ...?

    a. $a_n = 8n + 4; n \in \mathbb{N}$
    b. $a_n = 4n + 4; n \in \mathbb{N}$
    c. $a_n = n + 8; n \in \mathbb{N}$
    d. $a_n = 8n; n \in \mathbb{N}$

33. Dylan mows $\frac{2}{5}$ of the lawn. Then, he mows an additional area $\frac{2}{5}$ the size of what he just mowed. Next, he mows another area $\frac{2}{5}$ as large as the previous one. As he continues the process to infinity, what is the limit of the mowed area of the lawn?

    a. $\frac{3}{5}$
    b. $\frac{4}{5}$
    c. $\frac{2}{3}$
    d. $\frac{1}{2}$

34. Which of the following functions converges?

    a. $f(x) = 6x - 6$
    b. $f(x) = 16$
    c. $f(x) = \frac{4x}{x} + 1000$
    d. $f(x) = \frac{3x^2+100}{x^3}$

35. Which of the following graphs represents the solution to $y > 3x + 1$?

a.

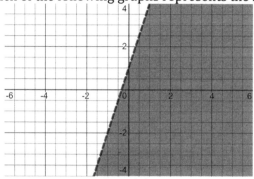

c.

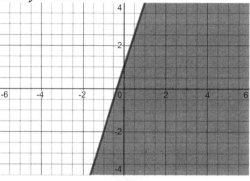

b.

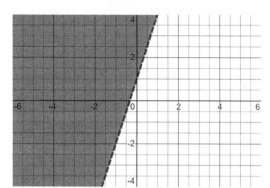

d.

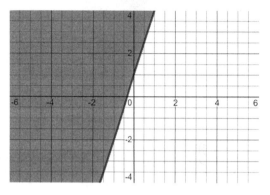

36. Which of the following tables contains points in an exponential function?

a.

x	y
−4	12
−1	−3
0	0
3	9
6	18

c.

x	y
−2	1/9
0	1
1	3
3	27
6	729

b.

x	y
−4	16
−1	2
0	1
2	1/4
5	1/32

d.

x	y
−4	−7
2	5
4	9
5	11
7	15

37. Given the graph below, what is the average rate of change from $f(2)$ to $f(6)$?

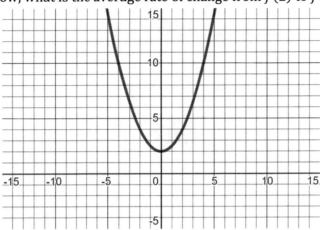

    a. 20
    b. 16
    c. 8
    d. 4

38. Jovan pays $130 for a hotel room, plus $24 for every person who will be staying in the room. Which of the following equations represents the cost?
    a. $y = 154x + 24$
    b. $y = 154x$
    c. $y = 130x + 24$
    d. $y = 24x + 130$

39. Which of the following is the graph of the equation $y = 3x - 2$?

a.
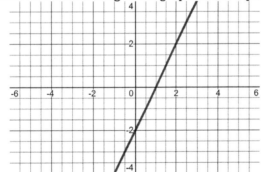

c.
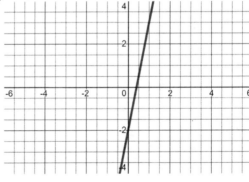

b.
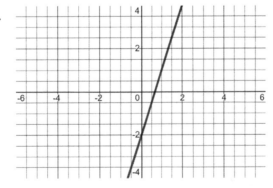

d.
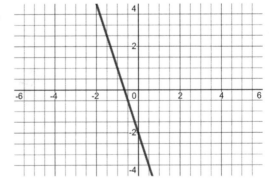

40. An apple falls from a high branch. The height of the apple is modeled by the function $f(x) = -x^2 - 2x + 7$, where $f(x)$ represents the height of the apple and x represents the number of seconds. Which of the following best represents the number of seconds that will pass before the apple reaches the ground?

    a. 1.8
    b. 2.1
    c. 2.3
    d. 2.6

41. A car moves at a constant velocity. Which of the following accurately describes the appearance of the position-time graph?

    a. It is a line with a positive slope.
    b. It is a line with a negative slope.
    c. It is a curve with an increasing slope.
    d. It is a curve with a decreasing slope.

42. What is the solution to the system of linear equations below?

$$-6x + y = 23$$
$$13x + 2y = 21$$

    a. $(-12, 6)$
    b. $(-1, 17)$
    c. $(1, 29)$
    d. $(12, 3)$

43. Mel is purchasing gifts for her students. She wants to buy stickers and notepads. She may purchase a maximum of 25 items and plans to spend at least $60. Each sheet of stickers costs $2 and each notepad costs $3. Which of the following graphs correctly shows the possible combinations of stickers and notepads that she may buy, assuming that the x-axis represents sheets of stickers and the y-axis represents notepads?

a.
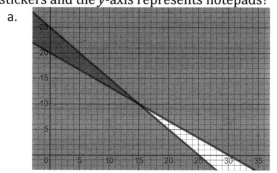

c.
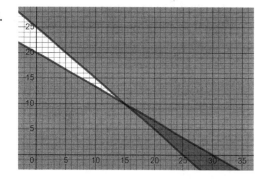

b.
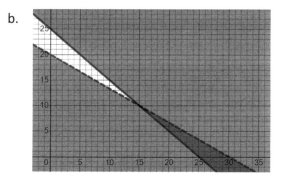

d.
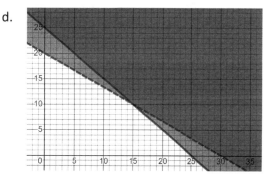

44. What is $\lim\limits_{n\to\infty} \frac{-n+7}{n}$?

    a. 7
    b. 0
    c. −1
    d. There is no limit.

45. Belle can buy 8 peaches and 3 bananas for $7.30. She can buy 3 peaches and 6 bananas for $4.20. How much does one banana cost?

    a. $0.30
    b. $0.45
    c. $0.65
    d. $0.80

46. The graph of the parent function $y = x^2$ is shifted 3 units to the left and 4 units up. Which of the following equations represents the transformed function?

    a. $y = (x - 3)^2 - 4$
    b. $y = (x + 3)^2 - 4$
    c. $y = (x - 3)^2 + 4$
    d. $y = (x + 3)^2 + 4$

47. What is the constant of proportionality represented by the table below?

x	y
−10	−5
−6	−3
−2	−1
0	0
4	2

    a. −2
    b. $-\frac{1}{2}$
    c. 2
    d. $\frac{1}{2}$

48. Zayn works out for 5 minutes per day for the first week. During each subsequent week, he plans to work out for 1.5 times as long as the previous week. Which of the following equations represents the length of his daily workout during the nth week?

    a. $a_n = 1.5n - 5$
    b. $a_n = 5 + 1.5^n$
    c. $a_n = 5 \times 1.5^n$
    d. $a_n = 5 \times 1.5^{n-1}$

49. Which of the following expressions is equivalent to $-5x(x - 1)^2$?

    a. $-5x^3 + 10x^2 - 5x$
    b. $-5x^3 - 10x^2 - 5x$
    c. $-5x^2 + 5x$
    d. $-5x^3 + 10x^2 + 5x$

50. Which of the following formulas may be used to represent the sequence $1, 6, 36, 216, \ldots$?

    a. $y = x^6$
    b. $y = 6^{x-1}$
    c. $y = 6x$
    d. $y = x + 6$

51. What is the sum of the first 40 positive multiples of 3?

    a. 615
    b. 1,230
    c. 2,460
    d. 4,920

52. Which of the following graphs represents an inverse proportional relationship?

a.

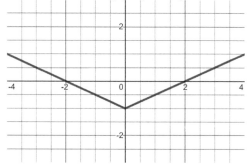

c.

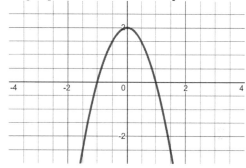

b.

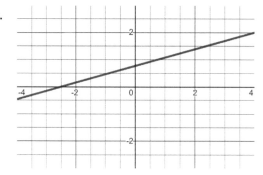

d.

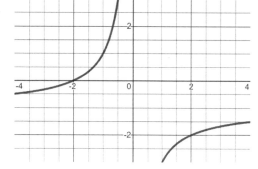

53. Which of the following graphs does *not* represent a function?

a.
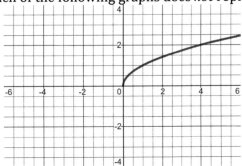

c.
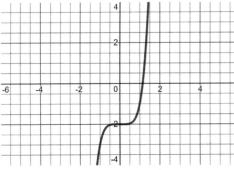

b.
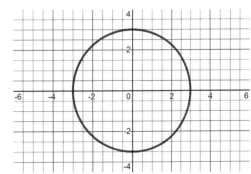

d.
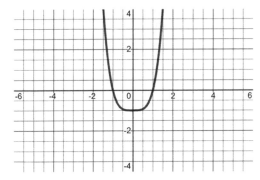

54. Raquel can paint a room in 4 hours. Melissa can paint the same room in 3.5 hours. If they work together, approximately how long will it take them to paint the room?

    a. 1.9 hours
    b. 2.1 hours
    c. 2.3 hours
    d. 2.5 hours

55. If $f(x) = \frac{2x^3 - 10x + 6}{3x}$, what is $f(3)$?

    a. $\frac{10}{3}$
    b. 10
    c. $\frac{10}{9}$
    d. 2

56. What is the derivative of $g(x) = x^{3m}$?

    a. $3m \times x^{3m-1}$
    b. $2m \times x^{2m}$
    c. $3m \times x^{2m}$
    d. $m \times x^{3m-1}$

57. Which of the following represents an inverse proportional relationship?

    a. $y = \frac{1}{x}$
    b. $y = \frac{1}{2}x$
    c. $y = x$
    d. $y = x^2$

70

58. Which of the following represents the graph of $y = (x - 1)^2 + 2$?

a.

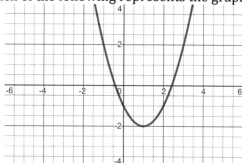

c.

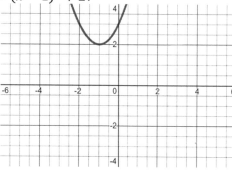

b.

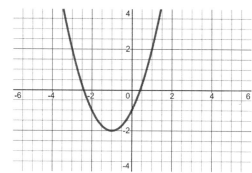

d.

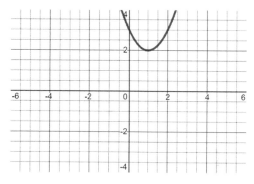

59. Mike is ordering a new polo shirt for each of his 12 employees, spending at least $150. Which of the following inequalities represents the possible costs?

    a. $150 < 12p$
    b. $150 > 12p$
    c. $150 \leq 12p$
    d. $150 \geq 12p$

60. What is the derivative of $f(x) = 6x$?

    a. 6
    b. $6x$
    c. $3x^2$
    d. $6x^2$

61. Which of the following represents a proportional relationship?

a.

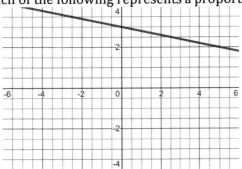

c.

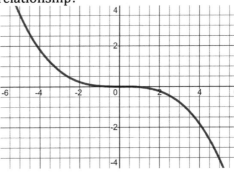

b.

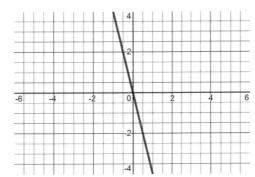

d.

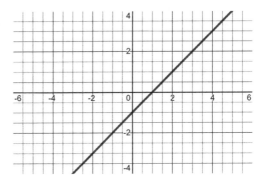

62. Carlos's monthly rent payment is represented by the graph shown below. The x-axis represents the number of months since beginning his lease, and the y-axis represents the total cost ($500 deposit plus $750 per month). Which of the following statements is correct?

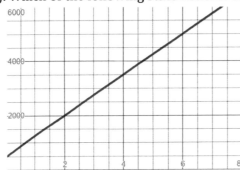

a. The cost is linear, but not proportional.
b. The cost is linear and proportional.
c. The cost is proportional, but not linear.
d. The cost represents an inverse proportional relationship.

63. Which type of function is represented by the table of values below?

x	y
−2	−4
−1	−0.5
0	0
1	0.5
2	4

 a. linear
 b. quadratic
 c. cubic
 d. exponential

64. What is $\lim\limits_{x \to -\infty} \dfrac{x}{x^2-4}$?

 a. 1
 b. $-\dfrac{1}{4}$
 c. 0
 d. There is no limit.

65. What linear equation includes the data in the table below?

x	y
−4	23
−1	11
3	−5
5	−13
8	−25

 a. $y = -4x + 7$
 b. $y = -3x + 11$
 c. $y = 2x - 15$
 d. $y = 5x + 43$

66. Evan plans to buy plants and ceramic pots. Each plant costs $7. Each ceramic pot costs $15. He can spend from $100 to $120. Which of the following inequalities may be used to find the combinations of plants and ceramic pots that he may purchase?

 a. $100 < 7p + 15c \le 120$
 b. $100 \le 7p + 15c \le 120$
 c. $100 \le 7p + 15c < 120$
 d. $100 < 7p + 15c < 120$

67. The variables x and y are in a linear relationship. The table below shows a few sample values. Which of the following graphs correctly represents the linear equation relating x and y?

x	y
−2	2
−1	1.5
0	1
1	0.5
2	0

a.
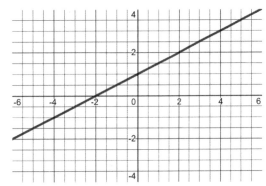

c.
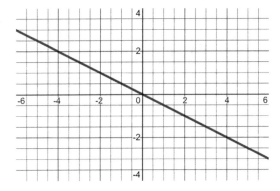

b.
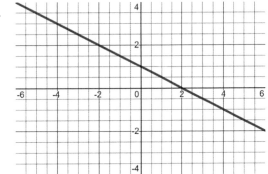

d.
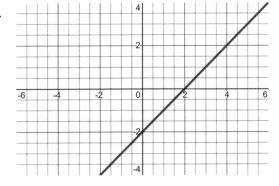

68. What is $\lim\limits_{n\to\infty} \frac{n^3-n^2}{n}$?

   a. 0
   b. 1
   c. 2
   d. There is no limit.

69. Which of the following equations represents a line perpendicular to the one graphed below and passing through the point (−3, 0)?

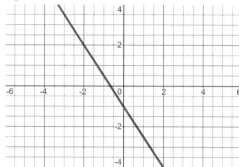

a. $y = -\frac{3}{2}x + 2$

b. $y = \frac{3}{2}x + \frac{1}{2}$

c. $y = \frac{2}{3}x + 2$

d. $y = 2x - 2$

70. Which of the following graphs represents the solution to the system of inequalities below?

$$-2x + 3y \leq 3$$
$$-8x + 6y \geq -3$$

a.

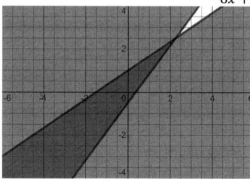

c.

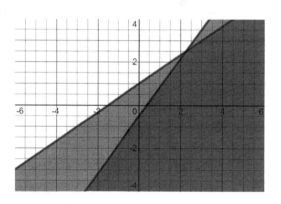

b.

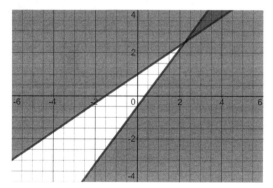

d.

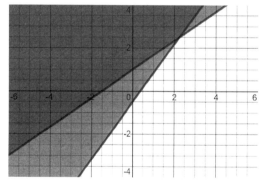

71. The expression $5x^2 - 3x - 14$ is equal to the product of $(x - 2)$ and which other factor?

a. $(5x - 14)$

b. $(5x - 3)$

c. $(5x + 7)$

d. $(5x + 14)$

72. Max sets aside a dollar of his paycheck this week. During each subsequent week, he plans to save 2 more dollars than he saved during the previous week. Which of the following equations represents the amount he will save during the nth week?

    a. $a_n = 2n - 1$
    b. $a_n = 2n + 1$
    c. $a_n = n + 2$
    d. $a_n = n - 1$

73. Which of the following equations represents a line parallel to the one graphed below and passing through the point $(-2, 2)$?

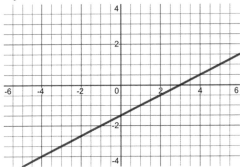

    a. $y = \frac{1}{2}x + 3$
    b. $y = \frac{1}{2}x - \frac{3}{2}$
    c. $y = -2x - 2$
    d. $y = -2x - \frac{3}{2}$

74. What is the solution to the system of linear equations graphed below?

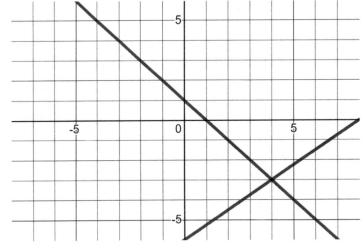

    a. $(0, 1)$
    b. $(2, -1)$
    c. $(4, 3)$
    d. $(4, -3)$

76

75. $g(x) = \frac{4-x}{x+6}$. What is the equation of the horizontal asymptote?

   a. $y = 0$

   b. $y = \frac{2}{3}$

   c. $y = -1$

   d. $y = -\frac{1}{6}$

Measurement and Geometry

76. What is the length of the hypotenuse in the right triangle shown below?

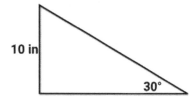

   a. $\frac{20}{3}\sqrt{3}$ in

   b. $10\sqrt{3}$ in

   c. 20 in

   d. $20\sqrt{3}$ in

77. Which of the following shapes is *not* a possible cross-section of a cone?

   a. circle

   b. rectangle

   c. ellipse

   d. triangle

78. A 24-foot-tall building casts a shadow that is 6 feet in length. If a dog next to the building casts a shadow 0.75 feet long, how tall is the dog?

   a. 1.5 feet

   b. 2 feet

   c. 2.5 feet

   d. 3 feet

79. Which of the following measurements is the best approximation of 1,982 square centimeters?

   a. 307 in^2

   b. 865 in^2

   c. 7,463 in^2

   d. 12,787 in^2

80. What is the distance on a coordinate plane from (−4, 6) to (0, −5)?

   a. $\sqrt{17}$

   b. $\sqrt{137}$

   c. $\sqrt{153}$

   d. $\sqrt{223}$

81. Zac eats $\frac{1}{9}$ of a bowl of chocolates. If the bowl contains $8\frac{4}{7}$ ounces of chocolate, how much chocolate does he eat?

    a. $\frac{59}{60}$ ounces

    b. $\frac{79}{80}$ ounces

    c. $\frac{20}{21}$ ounces

    d. $\frac{62}{63}$ ounces

82. What is the value of x, shown in the diagram below?

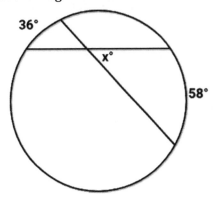

    a. 11
    b. 47
    c. 51
    d. 94

83. Given that the two vertical lines in the diagram below are parallel, which pair of angles is congruent?

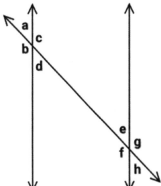

    a. ∠a and ∠g
    b. ∠b and ∠e
    c. ∠b and ∠g
    d. ∠e and ∠f

84. A can has a radius of 1.75 inches and a height of 6 inches. Which of the following best represents the volume of the can?

    a. 18.4 in^3

    b. 38.9 in^3

    c. 57.7 in^3

    d. 72.5 in^3

85. A box has a length of 22 centimeters, a height of 5 centimeters, and a width of 8 centimeters. How many square centimeters of plastic are needed to shrink-wrap the box?

    a. 560

    b. 652

    c. 748

    d. 880

86. A building is 44 feet tall and casts a shadow that is 59.2 ft in length. Which of the following best represents the distance from the top of the building to the end of the shadow?

    a. 39.6 ft

    b. 45.5 ft

    c. 61.9 ft

    d. 73.8 ft

87. What is the midpoint of the line segment below?

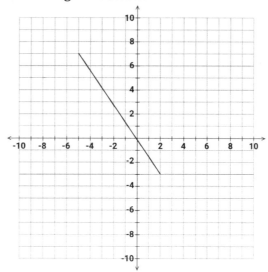

    a. (−1.5, 2)

    b. (−2, 3)

    c. (−2.5, 5)

    d. (−3, 3.5)

88. Given the diagram below, which of the following theorems may be used to verify that lines *a* and *b* are parallel?

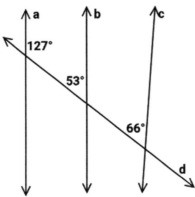

    a. Alternate Interior Angles Converse Theorem
    b. Alternate Exterior Angles Converse Theorem
    c. Consecutive Interior Angles Converse Theorem
    d. Corresponding Angles Converse Theorem

89. Which of the following transformations has been applied to the triangle in Quadrant I?

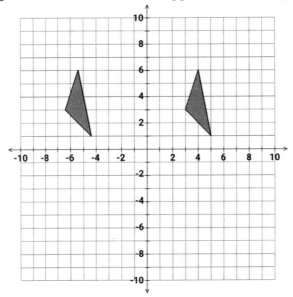

    a. translation
    b. rotation of 90 degrees
    c. reflection
    d. dilation

90. What is the approximate area of the shaded region in the figure shown below?

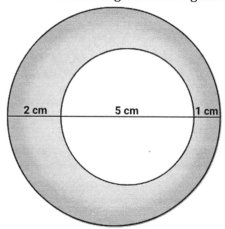

a. 28.7 cm^2
b. 30.6 cm^2
c. 32.4 cm^2
d. 35.1 cm^2

91. What is the value of x, shown in the diagram below?

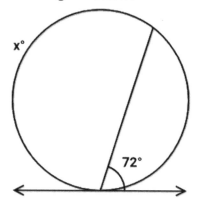

a. 36
b. 72
c. 144
d. 216

92. Which of the following pairs of shapes may tessellate a plane?
    a. regular pentagons and squares
    b. regular dodecagons and equilateral triangles
    c. squares and regular hexagons
    d. regular octagons and equilateral triangles

93. What scale factor was applied to the smaller triangle to obtain the larger triangle below?

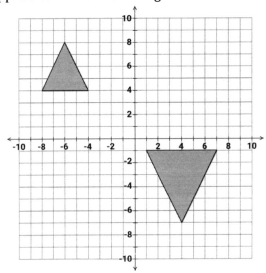

a. $\dfrac{1}{2}$

b. $\dfrac{2}{3}$

c. $\dfrac{3}{2}$

d. $\dfrac{5}{4}$

94. Which of the following pairs of equations represents the lines of symmetry in the figure below?

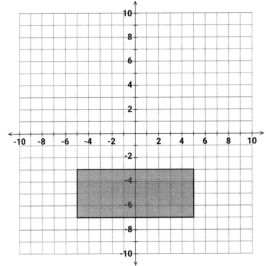

a. $x = 0, y = 5$
b. $x = 0, y = -5$
c. $y = 0, x = 5$
d. $y = 0, x = -5$

95. What is the slope of the leg marked x in the triangle graphed below?

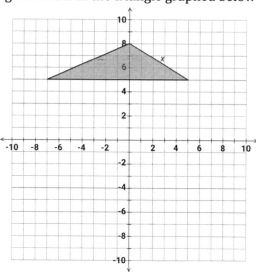

    a. –2

    b. $-\dfrac{1}{2}$

    c. $\dfrac{1}{2}$

    d. 2

96. What is the perimeter of the trapezoid graphed below?

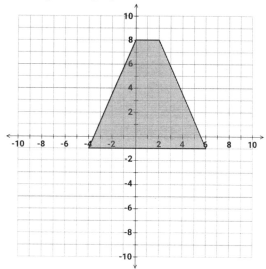

    a. $6 + \sqrt{97}$

    b. $8 + 4\sqrt{85}$

    c. $10 + 2\sqrt{85}$

    d. $12 + 2\sqrt{97}$

97. How many square feet of paint would be needed to cover a globe with a radius of 7.5 inches?

  a. 1.04
  b. 4.91
  c. 128.6
  d. 706.5

98. Which of the following postulates proves the congruence of the triangles below?

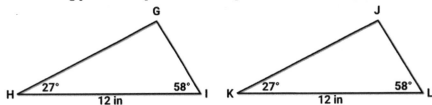

  a. ASA
  b. AAS
  c. SAS
  d. SSS

99. Which of the following steps were applied to the figure in Quadrant I?

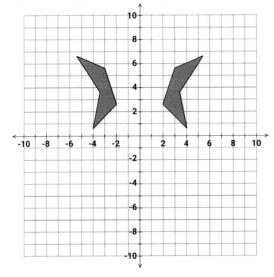

  a. reflection across the x-axis and rotation of 90 degrees
  b. reflection across the x-axis and rotation of 180 degrees
  c. reflection across the y-axis and rotation of 270 degrees
  d. reflection across the y-axis and rotation of 90 degrees

100. Which of the following best represents the measurement of x, shown in the right triangle below?

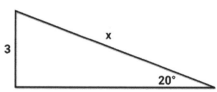

a. 8.8
b. 9.9
c. 10.1
d. 11.2

101. A city is at an elevation of 10,800 feet. Which of the following best represents the elevation in miles?

a. 0.49 miles
b. 1.95 miles
c. 2.05 miles
d. 2.98 miles

102. Given that $\overset{\frown}{MP} = 46°$ in the diagram, what is the measure of the inscribed angle $\angle MNP$?

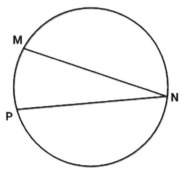

a. 18°
b. 23°
c. 38°
d. 46°

103. A convex three-dimensional figure has 8 edges and 5 faces. How many vertices does it have?

a. 4
b. 5
c. 6
d. 8

104. Each base of a triangular prism has a base length of 13 cm and a height of 15 cm. The height of the prism is 19 cm. What is the volume of the prism?

a. 1,572 cm^3
b. 1,684.75 cm^3
c. 1,775 cm^3
d. 1,852.5 cm^3

105. Given that the two horizontal lines in the diagram below are parallel, which of the following statements is correct?

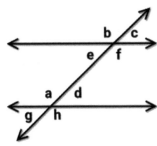

    a. ∠c and ∠g are complementary.
    b. ∠c and ∠h are supplementary.
    c. ∠a and ∠f are supplementary.
    d. ∠g and ∠h are congruent.

106. What is the area of the figure graphed below?

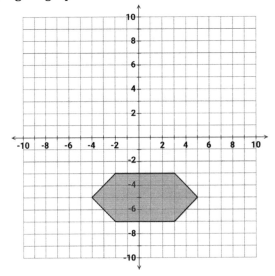

    a. 14 units^2
    b. 22.5 units^2
    c. 28 units^2
    d. 32.5 units^2

107. Which of the following represents the net of a tetrahedron?

a.

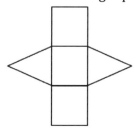

c.

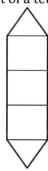

b.

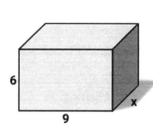

d.

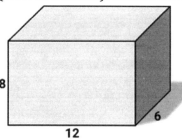

108. The two prisms shown below are similar (units are inches). What is the measurement of x?

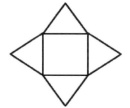

a. $4\frac{1}{2}$ in
b. $4\frac{3}{4}$ in
c. 5 in
d. $5\frac{1}{4}$ in

109. A ball has a diameter of 5 inches. Which of the following best represents the volume?

a. 65.4 in^3
b. 69.6 in^3
c. 72.5 in^3
d. 78.3 in^3

110. The figure on the graph below represents a triangular walking path, beginning and ending at point *x*. If each unit represents 0.25 miles, which of the following best represents the total distance of the path?

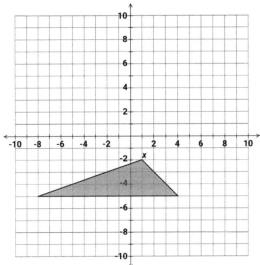

   a. 6.4 miles
   b. 12.2 miles
   c. 15.8 miles
   d. 25.7 miles

111. A trough is in the shape of an inverted square pyramid. If the base has a side length of 9 feet and the height of the container is 2.5 feet, how many cubic feet of water can the trough hold?

   a. 67.5
   b. 75
   c. 88.5
   d. 102

112. Which of the following postulates may be used to prove the congruence of $\triangle ABC$ and $\triangle DCB$?

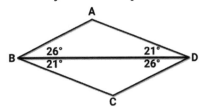

   a. ASA
   b. AA
   c. SAS
   d. SSS

Statistics, Probability, and Discrete Mathematics

113. Given the two-way frequency table below, which of the following *best* represents P(blue or felt tip)?

	Felt Tip	**Ballpoint**	**Total**
Black	3114	5283	8397
Blue	1756	2459	4215
Total	4870	7742	12,612

    a. 55%
    b. 60%
    c. 65%
    d. 70%

114. $A = \{3, 4, -3, 2, 6, 0\}$ and $B = \{-3, 2, 8, 1, 0\}$. What is $A \cup B$?

    a. $\{-3, 0, 2\}$
    b. $\{-3, 0, 1, 2, 3, 4, 6, 8\}$
    c. $\varnothing$
    d. $\{-3, 3, 0\}$

115. What is the converse of the statement below?

        If I see a robin, it is spring.

    a. If it is not spring, I do not see a robin.
    b. If it is spring, I do not see a robin.
    c. If I do not see a robin, it is not spring.
    d. If it is spring, I see a robin.

116. A business claims that the average employee works 1.2 overtime hours per week. A random sample of 30 employees shows an overtime mean of 1.4 hours and a standard deviation of 0.4 hours. Which of the following statements is true?

    a. The business' claim is likely true, as evidenced by a p-value less than 0.05.
    b. The business' claim is likely false, as evidenced by a p-value less than 0.05.
    c. The business' claim is likely true, as evidenced by a p-value greater than 0.05.
    d. The business' claim is likely false, as evidenced by a p-value greater than 0.05.

117. How many ways can the numerals 0–6 be arranged?

    a. 120
    b. 720
    c. 5,040
    d. 362,880

118. A student scores 72 on a final exam. Another student scores 90 on the exam. The class average is 84, with a standard deviation of 6 points. What percentage of the class scored within the range of these two students' scores?

    a. 61.08%
    b. 64.19%
    c. 66.87%
    d. 69.92%

119. How many ways can the top two performers be selected from a group of 5 candidates?

 a. 120
 b. 60
 c. 30
 d. 20

120. What is the area under the normal curve between ±1.5 standard deviations?

 a. approximately 87%
 b. approximately 90%
 c. approximately 95%
 d. approximately 99%

121. Using logic, when is $p \lor q$ true?

    I. When p is true but q is false.
    II. When q is true but p is false.
    III. When both p and q are true.

 a. I only
 b. I and II only
 c. III only
 d. I, II, and III

122. $A = \{6, 2, 2, 3, 5, 0\}$ and $B = \{2, 0, 3, 6, 9, 8\}$. What is $A \cap B$?

 a. $\{0, 2, 3, 6\}$
 b. $\{0, 2, 3, 5, 6, 8, 9\}$
 c. $\emptyset$
 d. $\{0, 9\}$

123. For which of the following data sets would the mean be an appropriate measure of center to use?

 a. $7, 7, 7, 10, 12, 13, 16, 17, 41, 42$
 b. $6, 12, 52, 52, 54, 57, 57, 59, 61, 65$
 c. $5, 8, 9, 9, 13, 16, 18, 19, 21, 21$
 d. $27, 28, 30, 30, 35, 38, 41, 41, 42, 1786$

124. Anne rolls a die and tosses a coin. What is the probability she gets a prime number greater than 2 or heads?

 a. $\frac{1}{2}$
 b. $\frac{2}{3}$
 c. $\frac{3}{4}$
 d. $\frac{5}{6}$

125. A student scores 93 on a test. The class average is 86, with a standard deviation of 5 points. What percentage of the class scored below this student?

 a. 89.99%
 b. 91.92%
 c. 96.87%
 d. 99.23%

126. What is the interquartile range of the data below?

   1, 2, 4, 8, 11, 14, 14, 18, 19, 23

   a. 8
   b. 10
   c. 12
   d. 14

127. Which of the following represents a tautology?

   a. $p \rightarrow (q \lor p)$
   b. $p \rightarrow (p \lor q)$
   c. $p \rightarrow (p \land q)$
   d. $p \rightarrow (q \land p)$

128. How many ways can you arrange the letters below, if order does not matter?

   STATISTICS

   a. 12,600
   b. 25,200
   c. 50,400
   d. 100,800

129. Matt rolls a die. What is the probability he gets a 2 or a prime number?

   a. $\frac{1}{4}$
   b. $\frac{1}{2}$
   c. $\frac{2}{3}$
   d. $\frac{3}{4}$

130. A student scores 90 on a test. The class average is 82, with a standard deviation of 5 points. What percentage of the class scored above this student?

   a. 4.79%
   b. 5.48%
   c. 6.32%
   d. 7.09%

131. A student scores 78 on a final exam. The class average is 84, with a standard deviation of 1.5 points. How many standard deviations below the class average is the student's score?

   a. 4
   b. 3.5
   c. 3
   d. 2.5

132. Using logic, when is $p \wedge q$ false?
    I.   When both p and q are true.
    II. When both p and q are false.
    III. When either p or q is true, but not both.

a. I only
b. II only
c. I and II only
d. II and III only

133. A manufacturer claims to include 24 ounces in each container of pasta, with a standard deviation of 0.35 ounces. A random sample of 25 containers shows a mean of 23.9 ounces. Which of the following statements is true?

a. The manufacturer's claim is likely true, as evidenced by a p-value less than 0.05.
b. The manufacturer's claim is likely true, as evidenced by a p-value greater than 0.05.
c. The manufacturer's claim is likely false, as evidenced by a p-value less than 0.05.
d. The manufacturer's claim is likely false, as evidenced by a p-value greater than 0.05.

134. What is the contrapositive of the statement below?

    If Lucy wears a scarf, it is winter.

a. If Lucy wears a scarf, it is not winter.
b. If Lucy does not wear a scarf, it is not winter.
c. If it is not winter, Lucy does not wear a scarf.
d. If it is winter, Lucy does not wear a scarf.

135. What is the limit of the series below?
$$1 + \frac{2}{3} + \frac{4}{9} + \frac{8}{27} + \frac{16}{81} + \cdots$$

a. 2
b. $2\frac{1}{3}$
c. $2\frac{2}{3}$
d. 3

136. Megan rolls a die and tosses a coin. What is the probability she gets a number greater than 5 and tails?

a. $\frac{1}{6}$
b. $\frac{1}{4}$
c. $\frac{1}{8}$
d. $\frac{1}{12}$

137. Which of the following describes a sampling technique that will likely increase the sampling error?

a. choosing every 4th person from a list
b. decreasing the sample size
c. grouping a sample according to age and then choosing every 7th person from the list
d. assigning numbers to a sample and then using a random number generator to choose numbers

138. Mark's nightstand currently holds 6 books, 12 pencils, and 1 highlighter. If he must place one item from each category in his backpack, how many possible selections are there?

  a. 19
  b. 72
  c. 144
  d. 180

139. Class A, with a total of 24 students, had a final exam average of 81 and a standard deviation of 6 points. Class B, with a total of 26 students, had a final exam average of 82, with a standard deviation of 5.5 points. Which of the following statements is true?

  a. There is no significant difference between the classes, as evidenced by a p-value greater than 0.05.
  b. There is no significant difference between the classes, as evidenced by a p-value less than 0.05.
  c. There is a significant difference between the classes, as evidenced by a p-value greater than 0.05.
  d. There is a significant difference between the classes, as evidenced by a p-value less than 0.05.

140. 75 students are surveyed. 36 of the students like only pepperoni pizza. 22 of the students like only supreme pizza. 12 of the students like neither kind of pizza. How many students like pepperoni *and* supreme pizza?

  a. 2
  b. 3
  c. 4
  d. 5

141. Which of the following best represents the standard deviation of the data below?

    23, 24, 26, 28, 31, 32, 35, 35

  a. 3.9
  b. 4.3
  c. 4.7
  d. 5.1

142. What is the size of the sample space for tossing three coins?

  a. 8
  b. 12
  c. 16
  d. 20

143. $A = \{0, -2, 1\}$ and $B = \{-1, 5, 4, 2\}$. What is $A \cap B$?

  a. $\{-2, -1, 0, 1, 2, 4, 5\}$
  b. $\{0\}$
  c. $\{-2, -1, 0, 1\}$
  d. $\emptyset$

144. A candy manufacturer claims to include 225 pieces in each bag. A random sample of 20 bags shows a mean of 223.5 pieces, with a standard deviation of 1.5 pieces. Which of the following statements is correct?

    a. The manufacturer's claim is likely true, as evidenced by a p-value less than 0.01.
    b. The manufacturer's claim is likely true, as evidenced by a p-value greater than 0.01.
    c. The manufacturer's claim is likely false, as evidenced by a p-value less than 0.01.
    d. The manufacturer's claim is likely false, as evidenced by a p-value greater than 0.01.

145. Julia rolls a six-sided die 300 times. How many times can she expect to roll a 6?

    a. 50
    b. 75
    c. 100
    d. 125

146. Given the boxplots below, which of the following statements is correct?

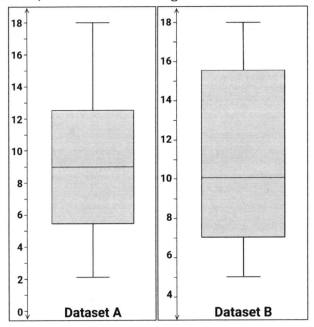

    a. Dataset A has a larger range and a larger median.
    b. Dataset A has a smaller range and a larger median.
    c. Dataset A has a larger range and a smaller median.
    d. Dataset A has a smaller range and a smaller median.

147. Which of the following statements is *not* true?

    a. In a skewed distribution, the mean, median, and mode are all different.
    b. In a positively skewed distribution, the mean will be to the right of the median.
    c. In a positively skewed distribution, the mode is greater than the median.
    d. The area under a normal curve is 1.

148. If the *x*-axis in the scatter plot below represents the number of miles Cyndi drives and the *y*-axis represents the gallons of gas left in her car's tank, which of the following is the *best* estimate for the number of gallons that will remain when she has driven 250 miles?

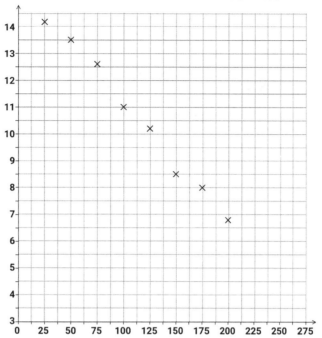

    a. 3.5 gallons
    b. 4.5 gallons
    c. 5.5 gallons
    d. 6.5 gallons

149. Jake rolls a standard six-sided die. What is the probability he rolls a number less than or equal to 5?

    a. $\frac{5}{6}$
    b. $\frac{1}{5}$
    c. $\frac{3}{4}$
    d. $\frac{1}{3}$

150. Which of the following is logically equivalent to $p \wedge q$?

    a. $p \vee q$
    b. $q \wedge p$
    c. $\neg q \rightarrow \neg p$
    d. $q \vee p$

Constructed Response

1. Shawna buys a new motorcycle for a purchase price of $9,800. The motorcycle will lose 20% of its value the day it is purchased and it will depreciate at a constant rate following that. The value of the motorcycle as a function of time can be modeled by $y = m - 0.08mx$, where y is the value of the motorcycle x years after it was purchased and m is the value after the initial 20% depreciation.

    a. What is the value of the motorcycle 4 years after its purchase date? Show your work.

    b. On an xy-grid, graph the value, y, of the car, as a function of x, where x represents the number of years after the purchase date, for $0 \le x \le 6$ years. Label the axes and show the scales used for the graph.

    c. Use your graph to estimate the number of years, x, after the purchase date that the value of the motorcycle is $6,000. Label this point on your graph and indicate the approximate coordinates of the point.

    d. Algebraically find the number of years, x, after the purchase date that the value of the motorcycle is exactly $6,000. Round your solution to the nearest tenth of a year. Show your work.

2. The diagram below shows a city square, where the city is installing new lights. The circles in the diagram show the areas that will be illuminated by the new lights. Each of the border lights has an illumination diameter of 12 feet and the center light has a diameter of 15 feet. The square has a diagonal of 80 feet.

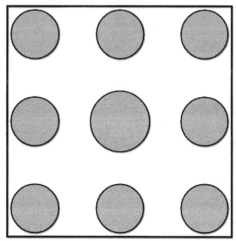

a. According to the diagram, what is the area that will be illuminated by the new lights? Show your work.

b. According to the diagram, what percentage of the square will NOT be illuminated by the new lights? Show your work.

c. If a ball were to fall on a random point within the square, what is the probability that the ball would fall in an illuminated area? Show your work or explain your reasoning.

3. Below are listed the final grades of the 18 students in a class.

    63, 71, 75, 78, 78, 80, 82, 83, 83, 86, 87, 89, 89, 91, 91, 93, 94, 99

a. For the numbers above, define and identify the median and the range.

b. Define and calculate the mean for the list of numbers above.

c. Draw a stem and leaf plot of the data using the tens digits as the stems and the units digits as the leaves.

Answer Key and Explanations

Number Sense and Operations

1. B: The 1 is in the tenths place, the 5 in the hundredths place, and the 8 in the thousandths place. Thus, 0.158 is equal to the sum of the product of 1 and $\frac{1}{10}$, the product of 5 and $\frac{1}{100}$, and the product of 8 and $\frac{1}{1000}$.

2. C: The repeating decimal may be converted to a fraction by writing:

$$10x = 8.\overline{8}$$
$$- \quad x = 0.\overline{8}$$

which simplifies as $10x - x = 8.\overline{8} - 0.\overline{8}$., or $9x = 8$.

3. D: The original price may be modeled by the equation, $(x - 0.3x) + 0.085(x - 0.3x) = 97.78$, which simplifies to $0.7595x = 97.78$. Dividing each side of the equation by the coefficient of x gives $x \approx 128.74$.

4. A: Multiplying two whole numbers will always result in a whole number.

5. A: The rectangular array represents the product of the side lengths of 4 and $(2 + 6)$.

6. A: The set of integers is contained within the set of rational numbers, and is hence a subset. A rational number may be written as the ratio, $\frac{a}{b}$, where a and b are integers and $b \neq 0$.

7. D: The sum is written as:

$$
\begin{array}{r}
1233 \\
+ \ 320 \\
\hline
2213
\end{array}
$$

The sum of 3 and 2 equals 5. In the base-4 number system, a number cannot contain any number larger than 3, so we rewrite it as 11 (1 four plus 1 one) and carry the 1 to the next column to the left. In this next column to the left, the sum of 1, 2, and 3 equals 6, so we rewrite it as 12 (1 four plus 2 ones) and carry the 1 to the next column to the left. The remaining digits can be added without exceeding 3.

8. D: The original price may be represented by the equation $158,400 = x - 0.12x$ or $158,400 = 0.88x$. Dividing both sides of the equation by 0.88 gives $x = 180,000$.

9. B: $p|q$ means that q is divisible by p, so dividing q by p will give an integer answer such as 6.

10. D: If $a < b < c$, it does not necessary follow that $ab < c$. For example, a could equal 3, b could equal 4, and c could equal 5.

11. B: The original cost may be represented by the equation $450 = x - 0.4x$ or $450 = 0.6x$. Dividing both sides of the equation by 0.6 gives $x = 750$.

12. D: The decimal point is 4 places to the right of the first digit, 4. Thus, $47,800 = 4.78 \times 10^4$.

13. A: First divide 4 into 129, recording the remainder. Then divide 4 into each resulting quotient, until the quotient is smaller than 4. Next, put the final quotient as the first digit. Then go backwards and write the remainders and place them as digits, in order from left to right.

14. D: The set of whole numbers is represented as $\{0, 1, 2, 3, \dots\}$. The set of counting numbers is represented as is represented as $\{1, 2, 3, \dots\}$. Thus the set of whole numbers includes all counting numbers plus zero, so the set of counting numbers is a subset of the set of whole numbers.

15. C: If the last two digits of a number, taken together, are divisible by 4, the entire number is also divisible by 4. For instance, in the number 2,716, we can see that the last two digits, 16, are divisible by 4 so we know that the entire number is divisible by 4.

16. A: If Yu is paid every 2 weeks, the following proportion may be written: $\frac{60}{2} = \frac{x}{52}$. We cross-multiply to obtain the equation $2x = 3,120$. Dividing both sides of the equation by 2 gives $x = 1,560$.

17. A: Kyra's monthly salary may be modeled as $\frac{1}{3}x = 1,050$. Multiplying both sides of the equation by 3 gives $x = 3,150$.

18. D: The commutative property of multiplication states that the order of multiplying two numbers does not matter: $a(b) = b(a)$.

19. C: The amount of time she spends on meals and homework is equal to $0.23(24)$, or 5.52, which is more than 5.

20. B: The total electricity cost is \$876.56. Thus, the ratio $\frac{127.56}{876.56}$ represents the percentage of electricity cost incurred during October. $\frac{127.56}{876.56} \approx 0.146$ or 14.6%.

21. C: The set of rational numbers includes any number that can be written as a fraction of two integers, where the denominator is not zero.

22. B: The amount she pays is equal to $0.001(3,200)$. Thus, she pays \$3.20.

23. B: The decimal expansion of an irrational number does not terminate or repeat. The number e is considered irrational because it does not terminate or repeat.

24. A: Dividing two integers may result in a quotient that is not an integer.

25. B: The percent increase is represented as $\frac{525-400}{400}$, which equals 0.3125 or 31.25%.

Algebra and Functions

26. D: The sum of an infinite geometric series may be modeled by the formula $S = \frac{a}{1-r}$, where a represents the initial value and r represents the common ratio. Substituting the initial value of 7 and common ratio of $\frac{8}{9}$ into the formula gives $= \frac{7}{1-\frac{8}{9}}$, which simplifies to $S = \frac{7}{\frac{1}{9}}$ or 63.

27. D: The situation may be modeled by the inequality $7.5x + 3y < 45$. Isolating the y-term gives $3y < -7.5x + 45$. Solving for y gives $y < -2.5x + 15$. Thus, the y-intercept will be 15, the line will be dotted, and a test point of $(0, 0)$ indicates the shading should occur below the line.

28. A: Evaluation of the expression for an x-value of -4 gives: $\left(2(-4)^3 - \frac{1}{2}(-4)^2 - 1\right)$, which equals -137.

29. D: The horizontal asymptote is equal to the ratio of the coefficient of $3x$ to the coefficient of $2x$, or $\frac{3}{2}$.

30. D: Relation D is the only one in which there is not any x-value that is mapped to more than one y-value. Thus, this relation represents a function.

31. C: As the denominator approaches infinity, the value of the function will get smaller and smaller and converge to 0.

32. B: The sum of 4 and the product of each term number and 4 equals the term value. For example, for term number 3, the value is equal to $4(3) + 4$, or 16.

33. C: The sequence $\frac{2}{5}, \frac{4}{25}, \frac{8}{125}, \frac{16}{625}, \ldots$, may be used to represent the situation. Substituting the initial value of $\frac{2}{5}$ and common ratio of $\frac{2}{5}$ into the formula $S = \frac{a}{1-r}$ gives $= \frac{\frac{2}{5}}{1-\frac{2}{5}}$, which simplifies to $S = \frac{\frac{2}{5}}{\frac{3}{5}}$ or $S = \frac{2}{3}$.

34. D: The expression can be broken down into $\frac{3}{x} + \frac{100}{x^3}$. The limit of each part of the expression is 0, so the limit of the entire function is 0. The function converges.

35. B: This graph shows a slope of 3, a y-intercept of 1, and the correct shading above the dotted line (line must be dotted since the inequality is greater than, not greater than or equal to). Using the test point $(0, 0)$, the equation $0 > 0 + 1$ may be written. Since 0 is not greater than 1, the solution is the shaded area above the dotted line, which does not contain the point $(0, 0)$.

36. B: The table represents part of a geometric sequence, with a common ratio of $\frac{1}{2}$, so it also represents points of an exponential function.

37. D: The graph shows $f(2) = 4$. Since the y-intercept of the parabola is 2, the following equation may be written: $4 = a(2)^2 + 2$, which simplifies to $4 = 4a + 2$. Subtracting 2 from both sides gives $2 = 4a$. Dividing both sides of the equation by 4 gives $a = \frac{1}{2}$. Thus, the graph represents the function $f(x) = \frac{1}{2}x^2 + 2$. Evaluating this function for an x-value of 6 gives $f(6) = \frac{1}{2}(6)^2 + 2$ or $f(6) = 20$. The average rate of change may be written as $A(x) = \frac{20-4}{6-2}$, which simplifies to $A(x) = 4$.

38. D: The slope is equal to 24, since each person costs \$24. The y-intercept is represented by the constant fee of \$130. Substituting 24 for m and 130 for b into the equation $y = mx + b$ gives $y = 24x + 130$.

39. B: Each of the graphs shows the correct y-intercept of -2, but only graph B shows the correct slope. Using the points $(0, -2)$ and $(1, 1)$, the slope of graph B may be written as $m = \frac{1-(-2)}{1-0}$, which simplifies to $m = 3$.

40. A: A graph of the function shows the positive x-intercept to occur at approximately $(1.8, 0)$. Thus, the ball will reach the ground after approximately 1.8 seconds.

41. A: The position of the car is changing according to a constant speed. Thus, the graph will show a straight line with positive but constant slope.

42. B: On a graph, the lines intersect at the point, $(-1, 17)$. Thus, $(-1, 17)$ is the solution to the system of linear equations.

43. A: The situation may be modeled by the following system of inequalities: $\begin{array}{l} 2x + 3y \geq 60 \\ x + y \leq 25 \end{array}$. A test point of $(0, 0)$ indicates shading should occur above the line for the top equation and below the line for the bottom equation. The overlapped shading occurs in the upper left portion between the lines. Thus, graph A represents the correct combinations of items that Mel may buy.

44. C: The limit is simply the quotient of $-n$ divided by n, or -1.

45. A: The situation may be modeled by the system $\begin{array}{l} 8x + 3y = 7.30 \\ 3x + 6y = 4.20 \end{array}$. Multiplying the top equation by -2 gives $\begin{array}{l} -16x - 6y = -14.60 \\ 3x + 6y = 4.20 \end{array}$. Addition of the two equations gives $-13x = -10.40$ or $x = 0.8$. Thus, one peach costs \$0.80. Plugging 0.80 into the top equation gives $8(0.80) + 3y = 7.30$, or $6.40 + 3y = 7.30$. We subtract 6.4 from each side to obtain $3y = 0.90$, or $y = 0.30$. So one banana costs \$0.30.

46. D: The sign of the constant, inside the squared term, is positive for a shift to the left and negative for a shift to the right. Thus, a movement of 3 units left is indicated by the expression $y = (x + 3)^2$. A shift of 4 units up is indicated by addition of 4 units to the squared term.

47. D: The constant of proportionality is equal to the slope. Using the points, $(0, 0)$ and $(4, 2)$, the slope may be written as $\frac{2-0}{4-0}$, which equals $\frac{1}{2}$.

48. D: This situation may be modeled by a geometric sequence, with a common ratio of 1.5 and initial value of 5. Substituting the common ratio and initial value into the formula $a_n = a_1 \times r^{n-1}$ gives $a_n = 5 \times 1.5^{n-1}$.

49. A: The expression $(x - 1)^2$ may be expanded as $x^2 - 2x + 1$. Multiplication of $-5x$ by this expression gives $-5x^3 + 10x^2 - 5x$.

50. B: The ratio between successive terms is constant (2), so this is a geometric series. A geometric sequence is represented by an exponential function.

51. C: The value of the 40th term may be found using the formula $a_n = a_1 + (n - 1)d$. Substituting the number of terms for n, the initial value of 3 for a, and the common difference of 3 for d gives: $a_{40} = 3 + (40 - 1)(3)$, which simplifies to $a_{40} = 120$. Now, the value of the 40th term may be substituted into the formula, $S_n = \frac{n(a_1 + a_n)}{2}$, which gives: $S_{40} = \frac{40(3 + 120)}{2}$, which simplifies to $S_{40} = 2{,}460$.

52. D: An inverse proportional relationship is represented by an equation in the form $y = \frac{k}{x}$, where k represents some constant of proportionality. The graph of this equation is a hyperbola with diagonal axes, symmetric about the lines $y = x - 1$ and $y = -x - 1$.

53. B: A vertical line will cross the graph at more than one point. Thus, it is not a function.

54. A: The situation may be modeled with the equation $\frac{1}{4} + \frac{1}{3.5} = \frac{1}{t}$, which simplifies to $\frac{15}{28} = \frac{1}{t}$. Thus, $t = \frac{28}{15}$. If working together, it will take them approximately 1.9 hours to decorate the cake.

55. A: Substituting 3 for each x-value gives $f(3) = \frac{2(3)^3 - 10(3) + 6}{3(3)}$, which simplifies to $f(3) = \frac{10}{3}$.

56. A: The derivative of an equation of the form $y = x^n$ is equal to $n \times x^{n-1}$. So the derivative of $g(x) = x^{3m}$ is equal to $3m \times x^{3m-1}$.

57. A: An inverse proportional relationship is written in the form $y = \frac{k}{x}$, thus the equation $y = \frac{1}{x}$ shows that y is inversely proportional to x.

58. D: This graph is shifted 1 unit to the right and 2 units up from that of the parent function, $y = x^2$.

59. C: Since he spends at least $150, the relation of the number of polo shirts to the minimum cost may be written as $12p \geq 150$. Alternatively, the inequality may be written as $150 \leq 12p$.

60. A: The derivative of an equation of the form $y = ax^n$ is equal to $(n \times a)x^{n-1}$. The exponent (n) in this expression is 1, so the derivative of $y = 6x$ is equal to $(1 \times 6)x^{1-1}$ or $6x^0$, which simplifies to 6.

61. B: The graph of a proportional relationship is a straight line that passes through the origin, or point $(0, 0)$.

62. A: The graph is a straight line that does not pass through the origin, or $(0, 0)$. Thus, it is linear but not proportional.

63. C: The points in table represent a nonlinear curve that rises toward the origin, levels off as it crosses, and then rises again. This is a cubic function.

64. C: As x goes to positive or negative infinity, only the leading term of a polynomial function of x matters. Therefore, we can ignore the "–4" in the denominator; $\lim_{x \to -\infty} \frac{x}{x^2-4} = \lim_{x \to -\infty} \frac{x}{x^2} = \lim_{x \to -\infty} \frac{1}{x}$. As x goes to negative infinity, $\frac{1}{x}$ approaches zero. The limit is therefore 0.

65. A: Using the points $(-4, 23)$ and $(-1, 11)$, the slope may be written as $m = \frac{11-23}{-1-(-4)}$ or $m = -4$. Substituting the slope of –4 and the x- and y-values from the point $(-1, 11)$ into the slope-intercept form of an equation gives $11 = -4(-1) + b$, which simplifies to $11 = 4 + b$. Subtracting 4 from both sides of the equation gives $b = 7$. Thus, the linear equation that includes the data in the table is $y = -4x + 7$.

66. B: Both inequalities will be less than or equal to, since he may spend anywhere from $100 to $120, including both of those values.

67. B: The table shows the y-intercept to be 1. The slope is equal to the ratio of change in y-values to change in corresponding x-values. As each x-value increases by 1, each y-value decreases by 0.5. Thus, the slope is $\frac{0.5}{1}$, or $\frac{1}{2}$. This graph represents the equation $y = \frac{1}{2}x + 1$.

68. D: We first factor the numerator: $n^2(n-1)$. We can then write the expression as $\frac{n^2(n-1)}{n}$, which reduces to $n(n-1)$. As the limit approaches infinity, both n and $n-1$ increase without bound, so the expression has no limit.

69. C: The slope of the graphed line is $-\frac{3}{2}$. A line perpendicular to this one will have a slope of $\frac{2}{3}$. Substituting the slope and the x- and y-values from the point $(-3, 0)$, into the slope-intercept form of an equation gives: $0 = \frac{2}{3}(-3) + b$, which simplifies to $0 = -2 + b$. Adding 2 to each side of the equation gives $b = 2$. So the equation of a line perpendicular to this one and passing through the point $(-3, 0)$ is $y = \frac{2}{3}x + 2$.

70. A: The test point of $(0, 0)$ indicates that shading should occur above the line with the steeper slope. The same test point indicates that shading should occur below the other line. The overlapped shading occurs between these two lines, in the lower left.

71. C: The product of $(x - 2)(5x + 7)$ equals $5x^2 + 7x - 10x - 14$, which simplifies to $5x^2 - 3x - 14$.

72. A: This situation may be modeled by an arithmetic sequence, with a common difference of 2 and initial value of 1. Substituting the common difference and initial value into the formula, $a_n = a_1 + (n-1)d$, gives $a_n = 1 + (n-1)2$, which simplifies to $a_n = 2n - 1$.

73. A: The slope of the graphed line is $\frac{1}{2}$. A line parallel to this one will also have a slope of $\frac{1}{2}$. Substituting the slope and the x- and y-values from the point $(-2, 2)$, into the slope-intercept form of an equation gives: $2 = \frac{1}{2}(-2) + b$, which simplifies to $2 = -1 + b$. Adding 1 to both sides of the equation gives $b = 3$. So the equation of a line parallel to this one and passing through the point $(-2, 2)$ is $y = \frac{1}{2}x + 3$.

74. D: The lines cross at the point with an x-value of 4 and a y-value of -3. Thus, the solution is $(4, -3)$.

75. C: The horizontal asymptote is equal to the ratio of the two coefficients of x, or $\frac{-1}{1}$, which equals -1.

Measurement and Geometry

76. C: The triangle is a 30-60-90 right triangle. Thus, if each leg is represented by x, the hypotenuse is represented by $2x$. Thus, the hypotenuse is equal to 20 in.

77. B: The cross-section of a cone will never be a rectangle.

78. D: The following proportion may be written and solved for x: $\frac{24}{6} = \frac{x}{0.75}$. Solving for x gives $x = 3$. Thus, the dog is 3 feet tall.

79. A: The following proportion may be written and solved for x: $\frac{2.54^2}{1} = \frac{1982}{x}$. So $(2.54)(2.54)x = 1982$. Dividing both sides of the equation by 6.4516 gives $x \approx 307.21$. Thus, 1,982 square centimeters is approximately equal to 307 square inches.

80. B: The distance may be calculated using the distance formula, $d = \sqrt{(x_2 - x_1)^2 + (y_2 - y_1)^2}$. Substituting the given coordinates, the following equation may be written:

$$d = \sqrt{\left(-4 - (0)\right)^2 + (6 - -5)^2}$$
$$d = \sqrt{137}$$

81. C: The amount Zac eats may be written as $\frac{1}{9} \times \frac{60}{7}$, which equals $\frac{60}{63}$ or $\frac{20}{21}$. Thus, he eats $\frac{20}{21}$ ounces of chocolate.

82. B: The measure of an angle formed by intersecting chords inside a circle is equal to one-half of the sum of the measures of the intercepted arcs. Thus, $x = \frac{1}{2}(36° + 58°)$, or $47°$.

83. C: $\angle$b and $\angle$g are alternate exterior angles. Thus, they are congruent.

84. C: The volume of a cylinder may be calculated using the formula $V = \pi r^2 h$, where r represents the radius and h represents the height. Substituting 1.75 for r and 6 for h gives $V = \pi(1.75)^2(6)$, which simplifies to $V \approx 57.7$.

85. B: The surface area of a rectangular prism may be calculated using the formula $SA = 2lw + 2wh + 2hl$. Substituting the dimensions of 22 centimeters, 5 centimeters, and 8 centimeters gives $SA = 2(22)(8) + 2(8)(5) + 2(5)(22)$. Thus, the surface area is 652 square inches.

86. D: The Pythagorean Theorem may be used to find the diagonal distance from the top of the building to the base of the shadow. The following equation may be written and solved for c: $44^2 + 59.2^2 = c^2$. Thus, $c \approx 73.8$. The distance is approximately 73.8 ft.

87. A: The midpoint may be calculated by using the formula $m = \left(\frac{x_1+x_2}{2}, \frac{y_1+y_2}{2}\right)$. Thus, the midpoint of the line segment shown may be written as $m = \left(\frac{-5+2}{2}, \frac{7-3}{2}\right)$, which simplifies to $m = (-1.5, 2)$.

88. C: The consecutive interior angles have supplementary angle measures, as 127° and 53° add up to 180°. According to the Consecutive Interior Angles Converse Theorem, two lines are parallel if a transversal, intersecting the lines, forms consecutive interior angles that are supplementary.

89. A: The triangle was translated across the y-axis. In translation, each point is moved the same distance and direction.

90. B: The area of the larger circle is equal to $\pi(4)^2$, or 50.2 square centimeters. The area of the smaller circle is equal to $\pi(2.5)^2$, or approximately 19.6 square centimeters. The area of the shaded region is equal to the difference of the areas of the two circles, or $50.2 \text{ cm}^2 - 19.6 \text{ cm}^2$, which equals 30.6 cm^2. So the area of the shaded region is about 30.6 cm^2.

91. D: The measure of the angle formed by the chord and the tangent is equal to one-half of the measure of the intercepted arc. Since the measure of the angle is 72°, the measure of the intercepted arc may be found by writing $72° = \frac{1}{2}x$. Dividing both sides of the equation by $\frac{1}{2}$ gives $x = 144°$. The measure of the intercepted arc may also be found by multiplying 72° by 2. Since the measure of the full circle is 360°, we subtract 144 from 360 to find that $x = 216°$.

92. B: Equilateral triangles and regular dodecagons may tessellate a plane. Each triangle may be attached to alternate sides of a dodecagon, leaving no gaps in the plane.

93. C: The smaller triangle has a base length of 4 units and a height of 6 units. The larger triangle has a base length of 6 units and a height of 9 units. Using the base lengths, the dimensions of the smaller triangle were multiplied by a scale factor of $\frac{6}{4}$, which reduces to $\frac{3}{2}$.

94. B: The vertical line of symmetry is represented by an equation of the form $x = a$. The horizontal line of symmetry is represented by an equation of the form $y = a$. One line of symmetry occurs at $x = 0$. The other line of symmetry occurs at $y = -5$.

95. B: The slope may be written as $m = \frac{8-5}{0-6}$, which simplifies to $m = -\frac{3}{6}$ or $-\frac{1}{2}$.

96. D: The perimeter is equal to the sum of the lengths of the two bases, 10 and 2 units, and the diagonal distances of the other two sides. Using the distance formula, each side length may be represented as $d = \sqrt{97}$. Thus, the sum of the two sides is equal to $2\sqrt{97}$. The whole perimeter is equal to $12 + 2\sqrt{97}$.

97. B: The surface area of a sphere may be calculated using the formula $SA = 4\pi r^2$. Substituting 7.5 for r gives $SA = 4\pi(7.5)^2$, which simplifies to $SA \approx 706.5$. So the surface area of the ball is approximately 706.5 square inches. There are twelve inches in a foot, so there are $12^2 = 144$ square inches in a square foot. In order to convert this measurement to square feet, then, the following proportion may be written and solved for x: $\frac{1}{144} = \frac{x}{706.5}$. So $x \approx 4.91$. It would take approximately 4.91 square feet of paint to cover the globe.

98. A: Two of the angles, plus the side between them, are congruent to the corresponding angles and side of the other triangle. Thus, the ASA (Angle-Side-Angle) Theorem may be used to prove the congruence of the triangles.

99. B: A reflection across the x-axis results in a triangle with vertices at $(2, -4)$, $(2, -7)$, and $(9, -4)$. A rotation of 180 degrees is denoted by the following: $(a, b) \rightarrow (-a, -b)$. Thus, rotating the reflected triangle by 180 degrees will result in a figure with vertices at $(-2, 4)$, $(-2, 7)$, and $(-9, 4)$. The transformed triangle indeed has these coordinates as its vertices.

100. A: The following equation may be written and solved for x: $\frac{\sin 20°}{1} = \frac{3}{x}$. Cross-multiplying gives: $x = \frac{3}{\sin 20°}$, or $x \approx 8.8$.

101. C: The following proportion may be written and solved for x: $\frac{5,280}{1} = \frac{10,800}{x}$. Thus, $x \approx 2.05$.

102. B: The measure of the inscribed angle is half of the measure of the intercepted arc. Since the intercepted arc measures $46°$, the inscribed angle is equal to $\frac{46°}{2}$ or $23°$.

103. B: The relationship between number of faces, edges, and vertices is represented by Euler's Formula, $E = F + V - 2$. Substituting 8 for E and 5 for F gives: $8 = 5 + V - 2$, which simplifies to $8 = V + 3$. Thus, $V = 5$.

104. D: The volume of a prism may be calculated using the formula $V = Bh$, where B represents the area of the base and h represents the height of the prism. The area of each triangular base is represented by $A = \frac{1}{2}(13)(15)$. So the area of each base is equal to 97.5 square centimeters. Substituting 97.5 for the area of the base and 19 for the height of the prism gives $V = (97.5)(19)$ or $V = 1,852.5$. The volume of the prism is 1,852.5 cm^3.

105. B: When two parallel lines are cut by a transversal, the consecutive angles formed inside the lines are supplementary.

106. C: The figure is a hexagon, which can be divided into two equal trapezoids. The area of a trapezoid may be calculated using the formula $A = \frac{1}{2}(b_1 + b_2)h$. Thus, the area of the trapezoid is represented as $A = \frac{1}{2}(9 + 5)(2)$, which simplifies to $A = 14$. We double this for the area of the hexagon. Thus, the total area is 28 square units.

107. D: The net of a tetrahedron, or triangular pyramid, has four triangular faces. So only D can be folded into a triangular prism.

108. A: Since the figures are similar, the following proportion may be written and solved for x: $\frac{8}{6} = \frac{6}{x}$. Thus, $x = \frac{36}{8}$ or $4\frac{1}{2}$.

109. A: The volume of a sphere may be calculated using the formula $V = \frac{4}{3}\pi r^3$, where r represents the radius. Substituting 2.5 for r gives $V = \frac{4}{3}\pi(2.5)^3$, which simplifies to $V \approx 65.4$.

110. A: The perimeter of the triangle is equal to the sum of the side lengths. The length of the longer diagonal side may be represented as $d = \sqrt{(1 - -8)^2 + (-2 - -5)^2}$, which simplifies to $d = \sqrt{90}$. The length of the shorter diagonal side may be represented as $d = \sqrt{(4-1)^2 + (-2 - -5)^2}$, which simplifies to $d = \sqrt{18}$. The base length is 12 units. Thus, the perimeter is equal to $12 + \sqrt{90} + \sqrt{18}$, which is approximately 25.73 units. Since each unit represents 0.25 miles, the total distance of the path is equal to the product of 25.73 and 0.25, or approximately 6.4 miles.

111. A: The volume of a pyramid may be calculated using the formula $V = \frac{1}{3}Bh$, where B represents the area of the base and h represents the height. Since the base is a square, the area of the base is equal to 9^2, or 81 square inches. Substituting 81 for B and 2.5 for h gives $V = \frac{1}{3}(81)(2.5)$, which simplifies to $V = 67.5$.

112. A: The two triangles are similar because they each have two congruent angles, and they share a side between the two angles. So the two triangles are congruent according to the ASA (Angle-Side-Angle) Congruence Postulate.

Statistics, Probability, and Discrete Mathematics

113. B: The probability may be written as $P(Blue\ or\ FT) = P(Blue) + P(FT) - P(Blue\ and\ FT)$. Substituting the probabilities, the following may be written: $P(Blue\ or\ FT) = \frac{4215}{12,612} + \frac{4870}{12,612} - \frac{1756}{12,612}$, which simplifies to $P(Blue\ or\ FT) = \frac{7329}{12,612}$ or approximately 60%.

114. B: $A \cup B$ means "A union B," or all of the elements in either of the two sets. "A union B" represents "A or B," that is, an element is in the union of A and B if it is in A *or* it is in B. The elements in sets A and B are –3, 0, 1, 2, 3, 4, 6 and 8.

115. D: If the statement is written in the form $p \rightarrow q$, then the converse is represented as $q \rightarrow p$. Thus, the converse should read, "If it is spring, I see a robin."

116. B: A t-test should be used. A t-score may be calculated using the formula $t = \frac{\bar{X}-\mu}{\frac{s}{\sqrt{n}}}$. Substituting the sample mean, population mean, sample standard deviation, and sample size into the formula gives $t = \frac{1.4-1.2}{\frac{.4}{\sqrt{30}}}$, which simplifies to $t \approx 2.74$. For degrees of freedom of 29, the p-value is approximately 0.01. Thus, there is a significant difference between what the business claimed to be the overtime average and what the actual sample average showed. The claim is likely false, as evidenced by a p-value less than 0.05.

117. C: Since there are 7 numerals, the answer is equal to 7!, or 5,040.

118. C: Two z-scores should be calculated, one for each student's score. The first z-score may be written as $z = \frac{72-84}{6}$, which simplifies to $z = -2$. The second z-score may be written as $z = \frac{90-84}{6}$, which simplifies to $z = 1$. The percentage of students scoring between these two scores is equal to the sum of the two mean to z areas. A z-score with an absolute value of 2 shows a mean to z area of 0.4772. A z-score of 0.5 shows a mean to z area of 0.1915. The sum of these two areas is 0.6687, or 66.87%.

119. D: This situation describes a permutation, since order matters. The formula for calculating a combination is $P(n,r) = \frac{n!}{(n-r)!}$. This situation may be represented as $P(5,2) = \frac{5!}{(5-2)!}$, which equals 20.

120. A: A z-score of 1.5 has a mean to z area of 0.4332, or 43.32%. Twice this percentage is about 87%.

121. D: Only when both p and q are false is the union of p and q false. So, I, II, and III are all correct.

122. A: $A \cap B$ means "A intersect B," or the elements that are common to both sets. "A intersect B" represents "A and B," that is, an element is in the intersection of A and B if it is in A *and* it is in B. The elements 0, 2, 3, and 6 are common to both sets.

123. C: Data sets A and B are asymmetrical: data set A is skewed toward lower values, and data set B is skewed toward higher values. This makes the mean a poor measure of center. Data set D is mostly symmetrical, but has a large outlier. The mean is very sensitive to outliers, and is not an appropriate measure of center for data sets that include them. Data set C is roughly symmetrical and has no outliers; the mean would be an appropriate measure of center here.

124. B: Since they are not mutually exclusive events, the probability may be written as $P(P \text{ or } H) = P(P) + P(H) - P(P \text{ and } H)$. Because the events are independent, $P(P \text{ and } H) = P(P) \times P(H)$. Substituting the probability of each event gives $(P \text{ or } H) = \frac{1}{3} + \frac{1}{2} - \left(\frac{1}{3} \times \frac{1}{2}\right)$, or $\frac{2}{3}$.

125. B: The z-score is written as $z = \frac{93-86}{5}$, which simplifies to $z = 1.4$. A z-score of 1.4 shows a mean to z area of 0.4192. Adding 0.5 to this area gives 0.9192, or 91.92%.

126. D: The median of the lower half of the scores is 4. The median of the upper half of the scores is 18. The interquartile range is equal to the difference in the first and third quartiles. Thus, the interquartile range is 14.

127. B: A tautology will show all true values in a truth table column. Look at the table below:

p	q	$p \wedge q$	$p \rightarrow (p \vee q)$
T	T	T	T
T	F	T	T
F	T	T	T
F	F	F	T

Only the statement $p \rightarrow (p \vee q)$ shows all T's in the column.

128. C: The number of ways the letters can be arranged may be represented as $\frac{10!}{3!3!2!1!1!}$, which equals 50,400.

129. B: Since they are not mutually exclusive events, the probability may be written as $P(2 \text{ or } P) = P(2) + P(P) - P(2 \text{ and } P)$. Substituting the probability of each event gives $(2 \text{ or } P) = \frac{1}{6} + \frac{1}{2} - \frac{1}{6}$, or $\frac{1}{2}$.

130. B: The z-score is written as $z = \frac{90-82}{5}$, which simplifies to $z = 1.6$. A z-score with an absolute value of 1.6 shows a mean to z area of 0.4452. Subtracting this area from 0.5 gives 0.0548, or 5.48%.

131. A: A z-score may be calculated using the formula $z = \frac{X-\mu}{\sigma}$. Substituting the score of 78, class average of 84, and class standard deviation of 1.5 into the formula gives: $z = \frac{78-84}{1.5}$, which simplifies to $z = -4$. Thus, the student's score is 4 standard deviations below the mean.

132. D: Both p and q must be true in order for the intersection to be true. So, I is incorrect but II and III are correct.

133. B: A z-test may be used, since the population standard deviation is known. A z-score may be calculated using the formula $z = \frac{\bar{X}-\mu}{\frac{\sigma}{\sqrt{n}}}$. Substituting the sample mean, population mean, population standard deviation, and sample size into the formula gives $z = \frac{23.9-24}{\frac{0.35}{\sqrt{25}}}$, which simplifies to $z \approx -1.43$. The p-value is approximately 0.15, which is greater than 0.05. Thus, there does not appear to be a significant difference between what the manufacturer claims and the actual number of ounces found in each container. The claim is likely true, due to a p-value greater than 0.05.

134. C: If the statement is written in the form $p \rightarrow q$, then the contrapositive is represented as $\neg q \rightarrow \neg p$. Thus, the contrapositive should read, "If it is not winter, Lucy does not wear a scarf."

135. D: The series is an infinite geometric series. The sum may be calculated using the formula $S = \frac{a}{1-r}$, where a represents the value of the first term and r represents the common ratio. Substituting 1 for a and $\frac{2}{3}$ for r gives $S = \frac{1}{1-\frac{2}{3}}$ or 3.

136. B: The probability may be written as $P(N \text{ and } T) = P(N) \times P(T)$. Substituting the probability of each event gives $(N \text{ and } T) = \frac{1}{6} \times \frac{1}{2}$, which simplifies to $\frac{1}{12}$.

137. B: Decreasing the sample size will likely increase the sampling error by increasing the likelihood of deviations from the true population. The other described techniques utilize random sampling.

138. B: This is a counting problem. The possible number of selections is equal to the product of the possibilities for each category. The product of 6, 12, and 1 is 72. Thus, there are 72 ways for Mark to fill his backpack.

139. A: A two-sample t-test should be used. Entering the sample mean, sample standard deviation, and sample size of each group into a graphing calculator reveals a p-value that is greater than 0.05, so no significant difference between the groups may be declared.

140. D: A Venn diagram may be drawn to assist in finding the answer.

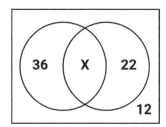

Since the set contains 75 total people, the solution is equal to $75 - (36 + 22 + 12)$ or 5 people.

141. C: The standard deviation is equal to the square root of the ratio of the sum of the squares of the deviation of each score from the mean to the square root of the difference of n and 1. The mean of the data set is 29.25. The deviations are –6.25, –5.25, –3.25, –1.25, 1.75, 2.75, 5.75, and 5.75. The sum of the squares of the deviations may be written as:

$$39.0625 + 27.5625 + 10.5625 + 1.5625 + 3.0625 + 7.5625 + 33.0625 + 33.0625 = 155.5$$

Division of this sum by $n - 1 = 7$ gives 22.21. The square root of this quotient is approximately 4.7.

142. A: The number in the sample space is equal to the number of possible outcomes for one coin toss, 2, raised to the power of the number of coin tosses, or 3. $2^3 = 8$.

143. D: The intersection of the two sets is empty, denoted by the symbol, Ø. There are not any elements common to both sets.

144. C: A t-test should be used. A t-score may be calculated using the formula $t = \frac{\bar{X} - \mu}{\frac{s}{\sqrt{n}}}$. Substituting the sample mean, population mean, sample standard deviation, and sample size into the formula gives $t = \frac{223.5 - 225}{\frac{1.5}{\sqrt{20}}}$, which simplifies to $t \approx -4.47$. For degrees of freedom of 19, any t-value greater than 3.88 will have a p-value less than 0.001. Thus, there is a significant difference between what the manufacturer claims and the actual amount included in each bag. The claim is likely false, due to a p-value less than 0.01.

145. A: The theoretical probability is $\frac{1}{6}$, and $\frac{1}{6}(300) = 50$.

146. C: The ends of Dataset A are farther apart (from 2 to 18 instead of 5 to 18), indicating a larger range. The horizontal line in the middle of a boxplot represents the median, so Dataset A has a smaller median (9 instead of 10).

147. C: The median is always greater than the mode in a positively skewed distribution.

148. B: The points may be entered into a graphing calculator or Excel spreadsheet to find the least-squares regression line. This line is approximately $y = -0.044x + 15.59$. Substituting 250 for x gives $y = -0.044(250) + 15.59$, or $y = 4.59$. Thus, 4.5 gallons is a good estimate for the amount of gas that will be left after 250 miles. If a line of best fit is predicted visually using the points (25, 14.2) and (100, 11), the slope between points near that line is approximately –0.043, and the line passes through the y-axis around 15. Thus, another good estimate would be 4.25. This estimate is also close to 4.5.

149. A: The number of outcomes in the event is 5 (rolling a 1, 2, 3, 4, or 5), and the sample space is 6 (numbers 1–6). Thus, the probability may be written as $\frac{5}{6}$.

150. B: The statement $p \wedge q$ is logically equivalent to $q \wedge p$ according to the commutative laws.

Constructed Response

1. A. First, according to the problem, m is the value of the motorcycle after its initial depreciation. The value drops by 20%, so:

$$c = \$9{,}800 - (0.2) \times (\$9{,}800) = \$7{,}840$$

Using this value for c and substituting it in, the value formula then becomes:

$$y = \$7{,}840 - (0.08) \times (\$7{,}840) \times (x)$$

Finally, solve for y when $x = 2$:

$$y = \$7{,}840 - (0.08) \times (\$7{,}840) \times (4)$$
$$y = \$7{,}840 - \$2{,}508.80$$
$$y = \$5{,}331.20$$

1. B. The graph of y will be linear since x is raised to the first power. Reordering the function to the $y = mx + b$ format, the y-intercept and slope are readily identifiable:

$$y = \$7{,}840 - \left(\frac{\$627.20}{year}\right) \times (x)$$
$$y = -\left(\frac{\$627.20}{year}\right) \times (x) + \$7{,}840$$

Thus, the slope is $-\$627.20$ per year and the y-intercept is $\$7{,}840$. Plotting this function looks like the following.

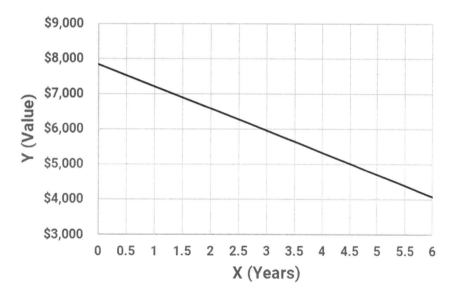

1. C. Using the axis values, it is readily apparent that the value function approaches $6,000 when x is around **3 years**.

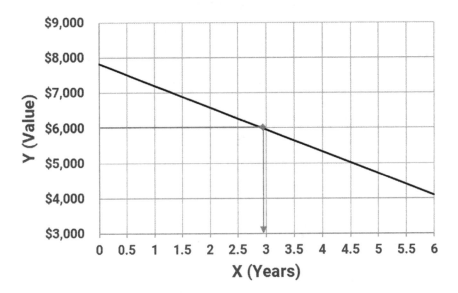

1. D. The way to use the function to find when the value is $6,000 is to substitute it in for y and solve for x:

$$\$6,000 = \$7,840 - \left(\frac{\$627.20}{year}\right) \times (x)$$

$$-\$1,840 = -\left(\frac{\$627.2}{year}\right) \times (x)$$

$$\frac{-\$1,840}{-\left(\frac{\$627.20}{year}\right)} = x$$

$$x = 2.934 \text{ years}$$

After rounding to the tenths place: $x = 2.9$ years

2. A. The illuminated area is the area of the 9 circles. The 8 circles on the border are all the same size. We can find their area by first finding the radius. Since the diameter is 12 feet, the radius is $\frac{12}{2} = 6$ feet. Thus, the area for the outer lights is given by:

$$A = 8 \times \pi \times r^2$$
$$A \cong 8 \times 3.14 \times (6 \text{ ft})^2$$
$$A \cong 904.32 \text{ ft}^2$$

Now we find the area of the larger interior circle. The diameter is 15 feet, so the radius is $\frac{15}{2} = 7.5$ feet. Thus, the area is:

$$A \cong 3.14 \times (7.5 \text{ ft})^2$$
$$A \cong 176.63 \text{ ft}^2$$

Finally, we add the areas of the 8 smaller circles to the area of the larger circle to get the total illuminated area:

$$A \cong 904.32 \text{ ft}^2 + 176.63 \text{ ft}^2$$
$$A \cong 1{,}080.95 \text{ ft}^2$$

2. B. To find the area that will not be illuminated, we need to find the total area of the square and subtract the illuminated areas (found in part A). First we need to find the length of the sides of the square. We know that the diagonal is 80 feet, and that drawing the diagonal across the square splits it into two 45-45-90 triangles:

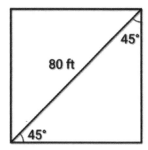

If we know the hypotenuse of a 45-45-90 triangle, we can find the legs by dividing by $\sqrt{2}$, so $\frac{80}{\sqrt{2}} \cong 56.57$ feet. Now we can find the area of the square:

$$A_{square} = s^2 \cong (56.57 \text{ ft})^2 \cong 3{,}200.16 \text{ ft}^2$$

Now we can subtract the illuminated area from the total square area to find the non-illuminated area:

$$A_{non-illuminated} \cong 3{,}200.16 \text{ ft}^2 - 1{,}080.95 \text{ ft}^2 \cong 2{,}119.21 \text{ ft}^2$$

The percent area is found by:

$$\frac{A_{non-illuminated}}{A_{square}} \times 100\% = \frac{2{,}119.21 \text{ ft}^2}{3{,}200.16 \text{ ft}^2} \times 100\% \cong 66.22\%$$

2. C. It can be assumed that a ball would have an equal chance of landing anywhere in the area of the square. Thus, the probability it will land in an illuminated area is given by:

$$P_{illuminated} = \frac{A_{illuminated}}{A_{square}} \cong \frac{1{,}080.95 \text{ ft}^2}{3{,}200.16 \text{ ft}^2} \cong 0.338$$

3. A. The median of a list of values is the centermost value of an ordered list. If the ordered list has an even number of members, then the median is the average of the two centermost values. The two center values in this list are 83 and 86, so we add them and divide by 2 to find the median. The range of a list is the difference of the highest value and the lowest value. Thus, for this problem, the median is $\frac{83+86}{2} = 84.5$ and the range is $99 - 63 = 33$.

3. B. The mean of a list of values is the sum of all the members of the list divided by the number of members in the list:

$$\text{mean} = \frac{63 + 71 + 75 + 2(78) + 80 + 82 + 2(83) + 86 + 87 + 2(89) + 91 + 91 + 93 + 94 + 99}{18}$$

$$\text{mean} = 84$$

3. C. The stem and leaf plot would look like this:

```
6 | 3
7 | 1  5  8  8
8 | 0  2  3  3  6  7  9  9
9 | 1  1  3  4  9
```

Thank You

We at Mometrix would like to extend our heartfelt thanks to you, our friend and patron, for allowing us to play a part in your journey. It is a privilege to serve people from all walks of life who are unified in their commitment to building the best future they can for themselves.

The preparation you devote to these important testing milestones may be the most valuable educational opportunity you have for making a real difference in your life. We encourage you to put your heart into it—that feeling of succeeding, overcoming, and yes, conquering will be well worth the hours you've invested.

We want to hear your story, your struggles and your successes, and if you see any opportunities for us to improve our materials so we can help others even more effectively in the future, please share that with us as well. **The team at Mometrix would be absolutely thrilled to hear from you!** So please, send us an email (support@mometrix.com) and let's stay in touch.

If you feel as though you need additional help, please check out the other resources we offer:

Study Guide: http://MometrixStudyGuides.com/NESINC

Flashcards: http://MometrixFlashcards.com/NESINC